Antonio Nieto-Rodriguez

Lead Successful Projects

BUSINESS

PENGUIN BUSINESS

UK | USA | Canada | Ireland | Australia
India | New Zealand | South Africa

Penguin Business is part of the Penguin Random
House group of companies whose addresses can
be found at global.penguinrandomhouse.com.

| Penguin
Random House
UK

First published 2019
001

Copyright © Antonio Nieto-Rodriguez, 2019

With thanks to LID Publishing for granting
permission for use of material from
The Project Revolution by Antonio Nieto-Rodriguez

The moral right of the author has been asserted

Text design by Richard Marston
Set in 11.75/14.75 pt Minion Pro
Typeset by Jouve (UK), Milton Keynes
Printed and bound in Great Britain by
Clays Ltd, Elcograf S.p.A.

A CIP catalogue record for this book is available
from the British Library

ISBN: 978–0–241–39547–9

**Follow us on LinkedIn: linkedin.com/
company/penguinbusiness**

www.greenpenguin.co.uk

MIX
Paper from
responsible sources
FSC® C018179

Penguin Random House is committed to a
sustainable future for our business, our readers
and our planet. This book is made from Forest
Stewardship Council® certified paper.

To my family, the most important
project in my life.
To my friends, who cheer and support
me along the way.
To those millions of project managers who
contribute in making a better world.

Contents

List of figures

Introduction

No matter what stage you have reached in your career, or which profession you work in, you will certainly have been involved in many projects – some of them successful, others less so. Projects are universal, but they can also be highly complex endeavours that require some basic elements to be in place in order to be successful. However, most of us have not received training in the methods and tools that are vital to project success.

This book's purpose is to fill that gap and provide you with an easy-to-apply framework – the 10 Principles of Project Success – to help you and your organization succeed in the new project-driven economy.

The principles are based on my years of experience and research covering hundreds of successful and failed projects, ranging from the smallest to the largest and most complex. The 10 Principles can be applied by any individual, team, organization or government, and are suitable for any kind of project.

The principles cover the fundamentals of projects that everyone should know, and are practical and easy to implement. They will assist you in leading projects – big and small – more successfully and in making your dreams a reality.

Each principle is explained in detail. I will give you tools and techniques to help you in the design, definition and implementation of any project you are involved in. You may decide to apply one principle after the other, or simply select those that your project might need to pay more attention to.

I recommend that you also use the principles as an evaluation checklist, either at the beginning or when the project is running. This will give you a sense of how well the project fundamentals have been taken into account, and whether the project has a good chance of being successful. It will also allow you to focus on what you really need to do.

This book provides you with the fundamentals required to be a successful project leader in today's fast-changing and project-driven world. I explain not only the skills and competencies needed, but also provide some guidance on how to acquire them.

More and more companies are focusing on building project implementation competencies. It has become a top priority for senior leaders. The last chapter explains how an organization, whether profit or non-profit, can put the 10 Principles to work. The end result can be personal and organizational transformation, leading to genuine change and the creation of project-driven organizations and project-savvy leaders.

I hope you enjoy, and learn from, reading this book, and that you put the ideas to work.

1 The emergence of projects

Projects help us reach our most ambitious goals. They can help us achieve more than we think is possible. There are few ways of working and collaborating that are as motivating and inspiring as working on a project that has a higher purpose, ambitious goals and a clear deadline. What people tend to remember most clearly from their working lives are the projects they worked on. Mastering the expertise to lead a successful project is becoming an increasingly crucial element of our professional skill set.

Research shows that project-based working is rapidly growing. One report by the Project Management Institute (PMI) found that the project management labour force is expected to expand by 33 per cent during the next decade. That means 22 million more project managers and a total project management workforce of 88 million by 2027. The value of economic activity worldwide that is project-oriented will grow from $12 trillion (in 2013) to $20 trillion (forecast 2027). That means millions of projects requiring millions of project managers every year. This silent revolution is impacting not only organizations but also the very nature of work, and our entire professional lives.

The project economy

The emergence of projects as the economic engine of our times is as silent as it is disruptive and powerful.

The project economy will be led by people. It will be led by people like you, tasked with the responsibility for delivering strategy and change that are likely to involve:

- new technology
- new ways of working across organizational (and geographical) boundaries, and
- new capabilities to learn, adapt and change.

You may already be a C-suite manager or a project sponsor, or you may be aspiring to this role.

Not so long ago, professional careers were made in only one or a handful of organizations. Throughout the twentieth century, most people worked for a single company, often solely in a specific domain, such as marketing or finance. However, research shows that the generation entering the workforce today are unlikely to remain with one company for extended periods of time, and retaining these workers has become a challenge for HR departments around the world. Today we are likely to work for several organizations and sometimes across numerous industries, and for part of our career we will most probably be self-employed.

LinkedIn co-founder Reid Hoffman believes that careers are now simply 'tours of duty,' prompting companies to design organizations that assume people will only stay a few years. And data bears this out: 58 percent of companies believe their new employees will stick around less than 10 years. (LinkedIn research shows that, on average, new degree-holders have twice as many jobs in their first five post-college years now as they did in the mid-1980s.)[1]

The growing trend in self-employment, noted by Quartz Media amongst others,[2] may see workers needing to take on a number of roles at the same time. And when they do, they will effectively be managing a portfolio of projects. This sort of career is best approached as a set of projects in which we apply the lessons we have learned from previous jobs, companies and industries while at the same time developing ourselves for our next career move.

What does the project career mean for employers and employees?

My prediction is that by 2025, regardless of the industry or sector, senior leaders and managers will spend at least 60 per cent of their time selecting, prioritizing and driving the execution of projects. Even the world's number one management thinker, Roger Martin, argues that 80 to 95 per cent of jobs in the senior management and corporate offices are an amalgam of projects. We will all become project leaders, no doubt about that!

In this new landscape, projects are becoming the essential model to deliver change and create value. In Germany, for example, approximately 40 per cent of the turnover and the activities of German companies are performed as projects. This is only going to increase.[3] Indeed, similar percentages can be found in most Western economies. The figures are even higher in China and in some of the other leading Asian economies, where project-based work has been an essential element in their economic emergence. The so-called gig economy is also driven by projects. Make no mistake, we are witnessing the inexorable rise of the project economy.

To succeed in that environment requires a whole battery of skills: from leadership, negotiating and decision making, to emotional intelligence, empathy, communication and political wiles.

The good news is that projects are human-centric and cannot be carried out by machines alone; they need humans to do the work. People must gather together around the purpose of the project, dividing up the work, establishing working relationships, interacting and addressing the social and emotional aspects of working together in order to generate high performance. Technology will, of course, play a role in projects – it will improve the selection of projects and increase the chances of success – but technology will be an enabler and not the goal.

The 10 Principles of Project Success

The purpose of this book is to provide you with an easy-to-apply framework to help you and organizations succeed in this new project-driven world. Having studied hundreds of successful and failed projects – ranging from the smallest to the largest and most complex – I have developed a simple framework that can be applied by any individual, team, organization or government.

While you may not necessarily be managing the project yourself, you need to understand the principles that underpin successful projects if you are going to meet the requirements of the task.

My 10 Principles of Project Success cover the fundamentals of projects that everyone should know, and are practical and easy to implement. They will assist you in leading projects, big and small, more successfully and in making your dreams a reality.

The 10 Principles of Project Success

1 **Everything starts with ideation**
Innovation, exploration, experimentation
Allow the time and provide the resources to imagine
before you establish the project

2 **A clear purpose informs and inspires**
Rationale, (dis)benefits, sustainability
Develop a simple purpose statement that articulates
both the problem and the solution

3 **The sponsor is both advocate and accountable**
Advocate, godparent, executive
Select a sponsor with the necessary level of belief
and skills and require them to provide sufficient
time and focus

4 **Customer needs drive the solution**
*Voice of the customer; definition, design and scope;
requirements and boundaries*
Put your customers at the front and centre,
and involve them throughout the project

5 **Realistic planning involves both ambition and
pragmatism**
Process, milestones, resources, cost
Temper your ambition with a realistic assessment of
the available resources, time and budget

6 The perfect is the enemy of the good
Test, assure, excel
Use your imagination to progress one step at a time
towards a successful outcome

7 Well-managed uncertainty is a source of advantage
Anticipate, monitor, mitigate
Ensure an approach to risk and uncertainty that
sustains a tension between pace and assurance

8 Stakeholder involvement is required and continual
Identify, communicate, engage
Start with an understanding of your stakeholders and
their understanding of the project and sustain this
throughout the process

9 A high-performing team and culture are indicators of the health and resilience of a project
Team, project, organization
Invest time to develop techniques to measure and
sustain your team's motivation, capability and
performance

10 Project-driven organizations build capability to deliver change
Selection, prioritization, implementation, agility
Design systems and processes for managing the
portfolio, developing project implementation
capabilities and aligning the organization

2 What are projects?

The word 'project' is extensively used, yet largely misunderstood. There is confusion about what is and isn't a project, as well as the nature of project management. So let's start by defining some simple terminology. Projects are limited in time; they have a start and an end. They require resources, often from different areas of expertise and backgrounds, bringing together people who have never worked together before. Projects are made up of a series of planned and costed activities, designed to deliver a new product or output, at least one element of which is unique. In other words, a project is something that has not been done before.

If a project delivers a defined outcome (a new product, a new piece of software, a new building, a new organization, etc.), a programme (or program) delivers capability; the organizational structures, processes, skills and knowledge that enable new behaviour. Programmes are composed of several, sometimes hundreds, of projects, and are much longer in duration.

The two activities are often combined. For example, the hugely innovative Swansea Bay Tidal Lagoon project, if it goes ahead, will create a tidal power station that generates dependable and sustainable power four times a day. It is also designed to create the engineering and logistical know-how that will allow the UK to build a further suite of five tidal power stations

Figure 1: New way of looking at a business

A simple model illustrates a new way of looking at an organization's activities, which shows the split between project and non-project activities and the relationship between the project and the organization.

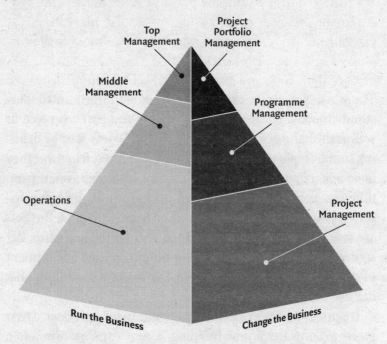

and transform other infrastructure projects through the development of techniques such as off-site manufacturing.[1]

Operations: Activities that run and keep the business alive

The core element of most organizations has traditionally been their operations, which include all of the activities involved in running the business. In a manufacturing company, these are supply, design, production, distribution, marketing and sales.

Operations are not only concerned with managing the production activities, or the plants, but also include the daily activities required to run the business, such as logistics, procurement, finance, sales, customer service, marketing, IT, payroll, etc. This component, which involves most of the employees and their worksites, is where management focuses most of their time and attention and is ultimately the source of the company's day-to-day revenue. Without operations, there is no business.

Since the 1920s, companies have been improving their operations as a means of increasing productivity by becoming more efficient, reducing costs and raising volumes and outputs. In the twentieth century, most companies were mainly producing goods – the service industry was not yet strong – and one of their main objectives was to grow. Growth by acquisition was not as popular as it is today. So growth was mainly organic, by increasing production capacity and by entering new markets. Once the industries became more mature, growth was achieved by increasing efficiencies and reducing costs. The impact of these growth techniques was that the number of projects increased over time.

Another important element that significantly influenced this trend was the fact that almost all the management gurus and their management theories focused on improvements for the run-the-business dimension. Frederick Taylor,[2] Henry Ford,[3] Igor Ansoff,[4] Peter Drucker,[5] Michael Porter[6] and other key influencers' recommendations were focused on improving the operations of the business. All of these activities were carried out as projects. These were often designed as one-off projects, but since changing a business involves carrying out a project, there was (and still is) no other effective way of managing them.

The result of all of these productivity changes is that companies in the twenty-first century have made their operations extremely efficient, reaching levels where finding additional improvements is no longer possible.

But just when organizations appeared to have things under control, a host of highly disruptive events and trends arrived. Today every organization, public or private, operates in an environment subject to continual and sometimes disruptive levels of change. There is political change, which can expose a business to new sources of competition. Markets may be opened or closed. New game-changing regulations may be introduced without warning. And there is, obviously, technological change, particularly associated with the internet and digital technology. To this can be added social change, with fluid customer attitudes towards the environment, health or social responsibility. Growing the business, boosting its profitability, or in some cases securing its continuation, heavily depends on anticipating, managing and, in many cases, driving change – which, in turn, depends on initiating and successfully completing projects.

Projects: Initiatives that change the business

Projects are the activities that change the business to ensure it is sustainable, and successful, in the mid and long term. They differ from daily operations in the following ways.

- Projects are one-off investments designed to achieve predetermined objectives.

- Projects are restricted in terms of time and budget and are staffed with temporary team members.
- Projects need different types of resources than operations. Project leaders need to work across sectors to bring different views together and thus require diplomacy and negotiation skills. They also need to be good at managing uncertainty, because large strategic projects are unpredictable.

After a project has been completed, the end product or outcome is often transferred to the operations side of the business, where the anticipated benefits must be successfully achieved. In the context of public projects, realizing the anticipated benefits of the project often depends on the citizen. For example, a project that develops a new online application for citizens to submit their tax returns digitally will only be successful if it is correctly managed by the tax department, and sufficient numbers of citizens embrace the new service.

Protecting the pipeline

Besides actually running the projects, a company needs to have a good overview of the pipeline of potential new ideas or investment opportunities, and the value they might bring to the business. Management usually decides to invest in a few ideas, but it is also very important to keep some in the pipeline. Monitoring and managing the ideas helps management react quickly to changes in the market, either in a defensive or a proactive way.

In many ways, managing the pipeline can prove as challenging as running the projects themselves. It is a process called 'portfolio management'. In organizations of any size, this requires a separate management function such as a project portfolio office or project management office, as well as a range of discrete processes and measures for assessing, distinguishing between projects and balancing them against each other in terms of:

- the investment and resources required
- the benefits anticipated
- the speed of delivery, and
- the associated risk.

As well as ranking projects, the portfolio team are responsible for assuring the selected projects all tie into the organization's declared strategy.

Overseeing the portfolio

The last yet most important piece for an organization is the oversight of the entire portfolio of projects. Large businesses have hundreds, sometimes thousands, of projects running in parallel.

Managing an organization's portfolio of projects means establishing processes and strong governance around:

- selecting and prioritizing projects in which to invest
- matching the requirements of projects to available investment and resources, and
- ensuring a balance between higher- and lower-risk projects, complex and simple projects.

All of this needs to be carried out within the context of a shifting external environment.

Things to consider before taking on a project

There are two additional elements I would like to highlight.

Project management has a cost

First, project management has a cost. Always. It adds a layer of overheads and oversight to the implementation of a number of activities. It requires resources and time (in the form of extra meetings and decisions), which contribute to the cost for an organization. According to studies, the project management costs for all phases of a project generally total somewhere between 7 per cent and 11 per cent of the project's total cost. If additional project controls are added, such as external audits, project management costs will be in the 9 per cent to 15 per cent range.

Project managers on small projects usually end up doing some or most of the project work. Blurring the lines between managing the project and completing the activities makes it difficult to identify the costs of management but usually allows for a pragmatic and economic approach to delivery. A larger degree of project management can be justified for medium-sized projects, and the largest amount of project management should be applied to large projects, where the stakes rise along with the project's complexity and risk.

It is important to set some clear and objective criteria to establish the difference between a project and day-to-day activities or operations. I tend to be pragmatic and recommend defining a set of criteria. For example, in large organizations, the following criteria can be applied:

- size of the project in terms of budget (e.g. above 500,000 dollars or euros)

- size in terms of duration (e.g. between six months and two years)
- size in terms of team members (e.g. more than five individuals required to do the project; in project management terms, more than five full-time equivalents or FTEs)
- at least three units, departments and/or regions impacted (e.g. strategy, operations, marketing, legal, IT)
- linked to a strategic objective (e.g. 'to grow our retail business in South America').

Projects with a minimum of three of these criteria should be managed by professional project managers using project management processes, tools and techniques, including risk management. They also require setting up an appropriate governance structure and monitoring system.

There are two key factors that you should consider when looking at your list of projects.

- Classify as projects only those that meet certain criteria.
- Apply project management when the size and complexity of the project require it, and in appropriate measure. (Larger, riskier and more complex projects require greater levels of control and oversight. Obvious, I know, but it often doesn't happen!)

The move from project management to project leadership

The second additional element to bear in mind is an observable business trend: that what was previously seen as project management is now moving towards project leadership.

Over the past thirty years, there has been a steady shift in focus from the hard-technical elements of projects and project management (such as scheduling, scoping, finance and risks) to the softer elements (such as people, behaviour, culture, communication and change).

We will see later the skills required to implement a project, but the leadership element is becoming increasingly relevant to assure not just delivery but a successful outcome.

3 Reinventing project management

Imagine a world in which most projects deliver the outcome that is intended. That may sound counter-intuitive? Projects are designed to deliver benefits, that's the whole point. However, there seems to be an impossible tension between the ever-increasing number of projects that organizations and governments are initiating – their growing scale and complexity – and the stubbornly poor performance of much of our project management.

There is work to be done. Even though, as we have seen, project management is universal and timeless, the statistics are not encouraging.

- According to research by IBM, '44 per cent of all projects failed to meet either time, budget or quality goals, while 15 per cent either stop or fail to meet all objectives.'[1]
- Geneca's 2017 study found that '75 per cent of respondents admit that their projects are either always or usually "doomed right from the start"'.[2]

The *Harvard Business Review* explains:

Managers use project plans, timelines, and budgets
to reduce what we call 'execution risk' – the risk that

designated activities won't be carried out properly – but they inevitably neglect these two other critical risks – the 'white space risk' that some required activities won't be identified in advance, leaving gaps in the project plan, and the 'integration risk' that the disparate activities won't come together at the end. So project teams can execute their tasks flawlessly, on time and under budget, and yet the overall project may still fail to deliver the intended results.[3]

This last example is particularly disheartening because it suggests that many otherwise good projects that are apparently 'well managed' still fail to deliver success.

The reasons for project failures

If we look at individual project failures, there is plenty that seems to go wrong. Let's take a look at some of the most notorious cases.

Budapest M4 metro

Originally conceived in 1972 as a means for transporting commuters between Budafok (south-west Budapest) and downtown Pest, the decision to build the Budapest M4 metro was made in May 1991 during the first Demszky administration. Nol.hu writes that the project was started without permits, without the consent of owners, without the necessary management and without money. With the exception of the deadline for completing the first section set by Demszky's successor, István Tarlós, not a single deadline was met.[4] The estimated final cost is around 3.5 times the original budget.

In project terms, the Budapest Metro almost feels like an anti-project as it seems to have broken all the rules. No proper project initiation documents (business case, scope, risk management plan), not even a budget and schedule. The Government simply agreed to act as guarantor for the finance. Big projects are often criticized for unrealistic schedules or hugely over-optimistic budgets but the solution is not simply to dispense with these elements. They are essential in framing the resources, the time-scale and what exactly will be built. Without a basic plan any big project will just grow and spread but is unlikely ever to finish.

Lesson: even the biggest of projects needs to start with the basics: a clear purpose and a coherent business plan. Who will do what, by when and for how much, with what anticipated result?

Saint Helena Airport

In 2010, the UK Department of International Development pumped $347 million (£285m) into building an ill-advised clifftop airport on the island of Saint Helena, a remote British territory in the middle of the Atlantic, with a view to boosting the island's accessibility and untapped tourism industry. Unfortunately, the level of wind shear makes it impossible for aircraft to take off or land safely.[5]

Success in any project is basically a mix of two things: what you are trying to do (the strategy) and how you are trying to do it (the project management). Government projects may be more prone to failure than commercial projects because governments are sometimes required to deliver projects that no sensible business would ever attempt. However, in this case, the project seems to have failed because of the lack of a coherent, deliverable strategy. a) Was it ever realistic to see Saint Helena as a tourist destination? And b) That question notwithstanding, delivering a practical airport was simply impossible because of the meteorology of the area.

Lesson: Make sure you take time to sense-check the basics – particularly for the most complex and ambitious of projects.

Russky Bridge, Vladivostok, Russia

This project cost an eye-watering $1 billion and can handle up to 50,000 cars a day but simply connects the city of Vladivostok with Russky Island, which has a population of just 5,000. To say the bridge is under-used would be an understatement.

Perhaps it is unfair to signal this project out for criticism. It delivered exactly what was expected of it: an iconic bridge (when something far more modest would have served). Leaving aside the politics of this kind of decision, it highlights the value of good cost engineering and agile project management – two disciplines that encourage those delivering projects to 'keep it simple'.

Lesson: Don't deliver an aircraft carrier when a float plane will do; try fixing the problem with a ferry before you build a bridge.

Oil and gas megaprojects

EY's 2015 'Spotlight on Oil and Gas Megaprojects' reported that 64 per cent of the projects currently under way were experiencing cost overruns and 73 per cent were experiencing schedule delays.

Complex projects often have complex problems. The EY analysis highlighted a catalogue of failings in many of these projects, including:

- poor (or over-optimistic) estimating
- poor contracting practice (which creates an adversarial relationship between client and contractors), and

- poor contingency and risk planning (so the project is subject to disruption from policy and regulation changes, with no mitigation of that risk).

Lesson: Avoid the temptation to pin down a complex project to a schedule or a budget too early. Your estimates will be taken as gospel and the project will be blighted from then on.

International Space Station (ISS)

This orbital laboratory is a joint effort between Russia, Europe, Japan, Canada and the USA. The project was so complex and unwieldy that it was already four years behind schedule when it began in 1998, and its original estimated cost of $17.4 billion ultimately grew to $150 billion. So far, the ISS hasn't been as much of a success as NASA hoped.[6]

There are limits to what can be achieved through projects. At the same time, project success is rarely a simple matter of time, cost and scope. Undertaking hugely ambitious projects of this kind is inherently risky, but space exploration is really a 100-year or even a 500-year programme. Programmes – particularly long and complex programmes – are designed to accommodate different levels of success and even failure. The whole point is that these are projects that involve learning by doing and learning from failure.

Lesson: Complex projects are about learning from failure. Fail fast, learn fast.

Boston's Big Dig

Boston's grand plan to bury the city's central highway in a 5.5-kilometre tunnel was budgeted to cost $2.8 billion but ended up costing $14.8 billion. Begun in 1982, it was plagued by escalating costs, overruns, leaks, accusations of shoddy workmanship and substandard materials, criminal arrests and a death. Originally scheduled to be completed in 1998, it was finally completed in 2007. The *Boston Globe* estimated that the project will ultimately cost $22 billion, including interest – and that it won't be paid off until 2038.[7]

Despite the legendary cost overruns, this was a surprisingly well-planned and well-executed project, involving an experienced contractor. It is an example of how difficult and uncertain major construction projects are in large cities. Surprises included: 'The unexpected discovery of 150-year-old revolutionary-era sites and Native American artefacts was one surprise complication and source of delays, requiring approvals from yet another diverse set of stakeholders, including historical and preservation organizations and Native American groups.'[8]

Lesson: If you are running major projects, make sure your organization has a strategy for addressing tail risk – the kind of event with a minuscule statistical likelihood but earth-shattering impact.

Energiewende

This is a German energy project aiming to transition away from fossil and nuclear energies (closing all nuclear power plants by 2022) and towards green energies. In reality, the country has not seen its emissions of greenhouse gases fall since 2009. German households, though, have to bear astronomical costs. One study estimates that the Energiewende project will cost Germans more than €1.5 trillion by 2050.[9]

Energiewende is a great example of a transformational project; one that impacts all aspects of industry and society. The legacy costs of shifting from established energy systems based on nuclear and fossil fuels will always be high and on-going. Projects like this struggle when viewed through a purely economic lens; once you apply other measures, such as environmental and social capital, the picture changes.

Lesson: You need to have clearly defined the purpose of your project, and what really drives value, before you start.

The pitfalls of entrepreneurship

Similar stories can be found in the field of entrepreneurship. A startup is a project or, better, a set of multiple projects linked to the vision and ambition of the founder. Since its launch in 2009, Kickstarter, the leading crowdfunding platform for startups, has hosted more than 409,000 projects, raising more than $3.3 billion. About 147,000 of them, or 36 per cent, have been successfully funded. However, according to Kickstarter's own statistics, 63.75 per cent of startup projects funded have failed.[10]

And we are often not just talking about fiascos in terms of cost overruns or late delivery. It is even harder to quantify the unmet benefits, social impact and loss of revenues that result from the massive delays, or failures, caused by poor projects and deficient project leadership – let alone determine whether the initial estimated benefits were actually met.

What needs to change?

So how do we turn these statistics around? And what are the principles that could set the foundations for success?

From project managers to project revolutionaries

First, we don't need project 'managers', we need project 'revolutionaries': people in whom the skills and behaviours of project management are embedded and who are as wedded to the end goal as they are to the means of achieving it. Research proves that very few people receive an education that teaches them the tools and techniques needed to define and manage projects successfully.[11] As I have lamented, the leading business schools in the world, such as Harvard, MIT, Wharton, Stanford, IMD, INSEAD and the London Business School, don't teach project management as part of the core curriculum of their MBA programmes.[12] And yet we need this understanding of a) what is to be achieved, and b) how to get there, to be a fundamental part of the skills and understanding of the strategists and leaders within the organization. Strategy and delivery (projects) are integrated and mutually dependent, and should be part of executive development.

From running the business to changing the business

Second, we need to recalibrate *all* organizations by shifting power, resources and budgets away from simply 'running the business' towards 'changing the business', which is the remit of projects and programmes.

Efficiency gains in business operations started with mass production more than a hundred years ago, and the trend has continued progressively since. Fewer resources have been dedicated to business operations, year after year. Now, in order to grow larger, companies need more new products or more building sites – in other words, more projects.

This is a trend that is reflected in the evolution of the economy. Governments' and central banks' economic and monetary structures have a direct impact on the number of projects that organizations can run. The amount of money in circulation in the economy, the availability of 'cheap' money (i.e. low interest rates) and the velocity of the money (i.e. the average frequency with which a unit of money is spent) can be indicators of this shift. The more money there is in the economy, the more companies use it to invest in strategic projects. The lower the interest rates, the more companies borrow to invest in strategic projects. To explain this, we can look at the evolution of gross domestic product (GDP) over the past century in the UK,[13] making the following assumptions.

- In recession years (negative GDP), companies reduce their spending on projects.
- In years with no GDP growth, nothing changes.
- In years with growth (positive GDP), companies increase their spending on projects.

The impact of these increases or decreases is felt the following year. Figure 2 shows the results of this analysis.

Figure 2: Shift from day-to-day work (operations) to change activities (projects)

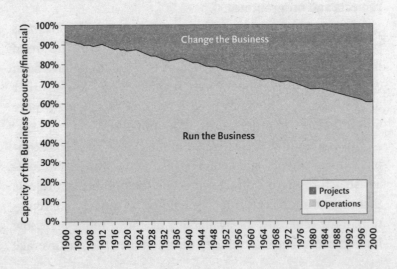

After decades of operational improvements, the opportunity for further efficiencies tends to be incremental rather than transformational. At the same time, the number of projects in organizations – their size, ambition, complexity and timescale – continues to grow unabated. Projects are on the march and, at the same time, the management models on which we used to rely as a basis for designing and running our businesses are now hopelessly inappropriate and outdated.

Yet, according to my latest research, more is to come. Disruptive technologies will accelerate this trend. Robots and artificial intelligence will take over almost all the traditional administrative activities and operational work. Some of these roles have already disappeared or been completely reshaped. Organizations will shift their focus more than ever to projects and project-based work. Projects are the new norm for creating value or, indeed, simply staying in business. We are now in the project economy.

The seven obstacles to project success

My research shows that the traditional functional company's poor project management skills and the resulting poor project performance can be linked to seven main obstacles.

1 Absence of uniform methods and standard processes
2 Misalignment of organizational structure with the company's changing reality
3 Lack of appropriate governing structure to support strategy execution
4 Lack of project execution culture, skills and leadership attention

5 Complexity of tracking and forecasting project costs, financials and benefits
6 Inadequacy of systems and tools for monitoring strategy execution
7 Lack of focus

1. Absence of uniform methods and standard processes

The existence of well-defined project management methods and processes – referred to as the project management 'methodology' – identifies those companies that have the best chance to consistently deliver project results.

For many decades, companies lacked a common and standard approach for managing projects, let alone a common definition. Projects were often initiated without a detailed business plan. Their costs were not only poorly defined before they started but were not properly tracked once the project began. To make things worse, one department would often launch a new project only to find out subsequently that another department within the same company had launched a similar project. With no uniform methodology or processes, companies were unable to effectively execute and document key aspects of a project.

Alongside this absence of project management methodology, companies lacked a standard way of selecting and prioritizing project ideas – which in project management terms is called 'project portfolio management' and is the engine for the change-the-business activities. This includes selecting those projects in which to invest, ensuring that they:

- are aligned to the company's strategy
- bring enough value to achieve the company's objectives, and
- are systematically executed until their completion.

It also includes deciding which initiatives to stop. A great example of a project being stopped is the decision by Airbus to stop the production of the largest passenger aircraft in the world, the A380.[14] Certainly it was not an easy decision to take after more than fourteen years, but probably the right one.

2. Misalignment of organizational structure with the company's changing reality

The alignment and the balance of the organizational structure need to reflect the shift towards change-the-business activities. More often than not, management underestimates or completely ignores this requirement; organizations fail to evolve (or adapt) as quickly as the business drivers, and consequently a large proportion of projects fail.

The departments in most functional organizations are not set up to work collaboratively. On the contrary, they suffer from internal competition and a silo mentality. Heads of departments invest in building their own little kingdoms Unfortunately, the largest and most critical projects are almost always cross-departmental.

Cross-departmental – or company-wide – projects in a traditional functional organization always raise the same fundamental questions.

- Which department is going to lead the project?
- Who is going to be the project manager?
- Who is the sponsor of the project?
- How are members selected for a multidisciplinary team in charge of a company-wide project, and how is their dedication to the project secured?
- Who is the owner of the resources assigned to the project?
- Who is going to pay for the project?

To summarize, almost all of the power in a traditional functional organization – meaning resources, budgets and decision making – still resides with the functional/department heads. But the most important projects have become cross-departmental, requiring the sharing of power among other members of the organization. For example, the integration of an acquired company, or a digital transformation, impact almost every business unit and function in an organization, requiring time and resources from most of them.

3. Lack of appropriate governing structure to support strategy execution

Another important reason why traditional hierarchical organizations have difficulty supporting and following up on strategy execution is the absence of the right governing structure. Today's organizations require a governing structure that includes a body to oversee the cross-departmental projects and provide a consolidated view of progress and problems across the portfolio.

A project management office (PMO), on the other hand, is a small department whose main mission is to follow up and to report on the progress of all projects under its scope. My recent research shows that 52 per cent of companies have an established project management department but only 23 per cent have a project portfolio management office, which is the engine that should coordinate the company's entire change-the-business dimension.

4. Lack of project execution culture, skills and leadership attention

Many companies lack a clear execution culture, an omission closely linked to the fact that many senior executives ignore the full potential of project management. This is typically reflected in the following ways.

- Project management not considered a core competency
- Absence of any career path for project managers
- Lack of training for senior management
- Failure to link incentives to project results
- Weak culture of accountability
- Inability to tackle cultural differences, silo mentalities and internal competition

5. Complexity of tracking and forecasting project costs, financials and benefits

What gets measured gets done, and what gets measured easily is much more likely to be deemed important. There is no disguising the fact that tracking project costs is extremely cumbersome in most organizational financial systems; measuring the benefits of investments is also a tortuous exercise.

Calculating precisely the time and resources that companies dedicate to change-the-business activities (projects) is a challenge. In most businesses, employees spend only part of their time working on projects and the rest continuing their operational work. A single individual may also work on several projects simultaneously. (The exceptions here are organizations such as consulting firms, which make a living completing projects, or companies that dedicate resources full-time to one specific project.)

Another problem with trying to accurately track project costs is that most companies outsource a portion of the project to external consultants or contractors, often for a fixed price. The method of recording these costs is different to that used to track employee costs. In addition, projects involve investment in software, hardware or equipment, many of which may be amortized by the business over a period of years and which may then be shared with subsequent projects.

Probably one of the biggest shortcomings in project management is the failure to track clearly the benefits delivered by projects. In principle, a solid project management culture should help a company achieve its strategic objectives. Yet, in reality, most of the project benefits as described in the initial business case are rarely tracked.

Finally, the standard annual budgeting cycle of many organizations simply does not correlate with the needs of its projects, which may run for a wide variety of funding periods.

Very few companies create a budget for company-wide change-the-business activities. Some companies forecast project costs by department, but rarely do they develop a budget for projects that are in the best interests of the entire company.

6. Inadequacy of systems and tools for monitoring strategy execution

Company shareholders, boards and even financial analysts rarely demand detailed information about the key projects and change-the-business activities once the investment decision has been made.

Neither of the two most important sets of accounting standards clearly specifies how companies should report on their projects and their change-the-business activities. Both the Generally Accepted Accounting Principles (US GAAP) and the International Accounting Standards (IAS) fail to include a codification topic covering how to account for project costs and how to report project benefits. The closest they get to mentioning project reporting is a discussion of development costs that should be amortized (US GAAP 350-50/IAS 38).

7. Lack of focus

Collectively, the problems associated with how organizations manage their portfolio and the projects within it may be described as a lack of focus.

- Top executives do not know the extent of the portfolio or understand the status of the projects within it.
- Being focused is difficult and requires discipline.
- Closing delayed projects (or those that are no longer relevant or drifting from their objectives) is very difficult, and consequently the number of projects continues to increase.

Moving forward

The fact is that the world will see an increase in project spending – an average $3.7 trillion in annual infrastructure spending between now and 2035 to keep pace with expected GDP growth[15] – yet the risk of project failure will continue to be huge, unless organizations and governments embrace advanced project leadership practices.

All is not lost. The good news is that there are many great examples of excellence in project management. The iPhone, the 2014 World Cup-winning German football team, the Airbus, the Panama Canal expansion, the Boeing 777, the Hong Kong–Zhuhai–Macau Bridge or the Renault–Nissan alliance are just a few.

What did these examples have in common? How did they successfully manage their projects? What lessons can we learn to ensure that, in the future, projects are significantly more successful, generate great wealth for the economy and impart benefits to our societies?

In the following chapters I am going to describe in detail a framework that can be used by leaders and organizations at the beginning of a project to assess how well it has been defined and whether it is worth starting right away or needs further refinement. This framework consists of principles that can be applied to programmes, strategic initiatives and any other activities that can be considered projects.

The 10 Principles of Project Success have been implemented successfully in several organizations (small, medium and large) in different sectors across the world, yielding significant tangible improvements both in terms of return on investment and in developing an execution-driven mindset and culture. The organizations include a leading European Bank, a pharmaceutical corporation, government institutions, a global cinema conglomerate with more than 100 theatres in Europe and North America and a US-based corporate law firm, one of the most prestigious in the world.

Let's start to take a look at how the 10 Principles work in practice.

4 Principle #1: Everything starts with ideation

Innovation, exploration, experimentation

Allow the time and provide the resources to imagine before you establish the project. Defining the project from the outset is a crucial part of the process. Ask yourself the following questions.

- What is it that you are going to deliver?
- What is the question for which your project will be the answer, and why?
- What are the various options you could select *before* you choose the one you will select?
- Is it the right time to start the project now?
- Do you have enough capacity, resources, management attention to dedicate to the project as an organization?

History is littered with projects that were very well managed but ultimately solved the wrong problem or it was realized, after an attractive business case had been made, that there was no problem or opportunity at all. Most organizations have the bad habit of launching a full-blown project for every idea they generate, producing a vast quantity of projects, most of which are a dead end and waste precious company resources.

One of the reasons for the explosion of projects in organizations is that starting projects is very easy, yet following through is what really makes the difference. In fact, one of the most frequently used words in organizations besides 'project' is 'kick-off'. After a discussion or a brainstorming session, it is common to hear someone – often senior management – saying, 'Let's make a project and plan a kick-off next week.'

Principle #1 opens, appropriately, with the project catalyst – why are you doing the project, what do you hope to achieve by it and what's in it for those involved? The answers to these questions will become the drivers of progress once the project gets under way. Ideation, exploration, experimentation, design thinking are key elements to be considered in order to ensure the success of projects, yet it is common practice to overlook them. In fact, current project management methodologies do not consider them as part of the standard project life cycle.

Ideation and exploration allow and encourage you to step out from everything you know and everything you have done before. There may be a radically new solution to your problem; hence the need to imagine. Exploration will also help you achieve buy-in and resources from the decision makers in your organization; to capture their attention and gain time from the executives. Imagining the project, its opportunities, obstacles and outcomes, from every perspective will enable you to engage members of the project team and secure support from anyone impacted by the project.

Experimentation permits trying out options and solutions without committing the organization to significant expenditure. Dedicate a few resources in small teams to prototype and test some of the concepts developed through the ideation and exploration exercises. The Lean Startup approach is a good source of inspiration.[1]

Not starting a project right away might give the impression that you are losing time, yet research says that projects that have a thorough exploration phase choose the best ideas and deliver the most successful and valuable projects.

Lessons from Project Purple – the iPhone

From the hundreds of projects I have analysed, a handful stand out. One of them is what in 2004 was coined as Project Purple, the creation of the iPhone. Since its debut release in 2007 the iPhone has become both a cultural and economic phenomenon; revolutionizing the idea of the 'smartphone', replacing BlackBerry and Nokia as the must-have business and personal device, and turning the entire global telecoms market upside down. And this from a company with no previous significant experience in the mobile industry!

According to one estimate, Apple spent $150 million developing the iPhone (excluding the cost of the ideation phase). That $150 million certainly ranks Purple Project as one of the best investments ever. 'There are very few products that have boosted the financials of a company in the way that the iPhone has for Apple,' says Ian Fogg, head of mobile at research firm IHS.[2] Apple sold 1.4 million iPhones in 2007 and more than 201 million units worldwide in 2016. In total, Apple has sold more than one billion iPhones worldwide from 2007 to 2016.

In the first quarter of 2017, iPhone sales accounted for more than 69 per cent of Apple's total revenue, with an estimated margin above 50 per cent, generating more than $54 billion in revenues. In ten years, Apple's revenue grew from $8 billion in 2004 to more than $215 billion in 2016.

What is noteworthy is that Apple didn't launch a formal and full-scale project to develop the first concepts for the iPhone.[3]

They applied this first principle: everything starts with ideation. The ideation phase was kept low profile, with limited investments and small teams experimenting with different concepts and ideas.

Like most Apple success stories, the iPhone can trace its roots back to Steve Jobs. Shortly after the first iPod was released in 2002, several members of the Apple executive team tried to convince Jobs that producing a phone was a great idea and they should launch a project. But Steve was sceptical and rejected it many times. Instead, he allowed some of them to experiment. There were as many as five different phones or phone-related initiatives – from tiny research endeavours to a flopped partnership with Motorola on the ROKR phone (which some described as the first iTunes phone)[4] – bubbling up at Apple by the middle of the 2000s.

It was only in 2004 – more precisely, it was late at night on 7 November 2004, after receiving an email from vice president Michael Bell, explaining why they really should make the phone – that Steve Jobs said, 'Okay, I think we should go do it.' Almost three years after the first idea of producing a phone, and after lots of ideation, exploration and experimentation.

On 29 June 2007, at the annual Macworld trade show, the first iPhone was released. That is just two and a half years to produce a revolutionary phone, the first smartphone, by a company that had not produced phones before. Just insane!

Lessons from the Google Glass

Google Glass is an optical display designed in the shape of a pair of eyeglasses; effectively a head-mounted wearable computer. It displays information in a smartphone-style hands-free format. Google started selling prototypes of Google Glass in the USA in April 2013, only to announce in January 2015 that it would stop production. What went wrong?

Google Glass was a project launched from a half-baked idea. The business case was assessed very poorly and wasn't as clear as it should have been.[5] First of all, Google should have defined and tested their assumptions in the real world before planning the launch. Google X, the radical technology arm of the business, failed to conduct proper market research and customer development. Google X assumed the world was ready to wear cameras on their faces but never validated that assumption. Google X also saw Google Glass as a great innovation but didn't invest enough critical thinking into sense-checking the real value it might deliver. Nor did they ask themselves whether users would be comfortable wearing a camera in front of their face every day?

This was, by any standards, a visionary and innovative project. But, beyond the basic requirements, there was unresolved confusion around the purpose of the device. Should it be worn all day, like a fashionable device or simply put on to fulfil specific functions? Google Glass could have been a transformational tool for professionals.[6] Truck drivers or aeroplane pilots, for example, could instantly access directions and reports to help them navigate, without lifting a finger. Machine operators, police, security personnel or physicians could all have gained a lot from the device. But instead of targeting professional and B2B audiences, Google limited access to a specific community of 'Glass Explorers' – journalists, techies and celebrities – and made them the priority target.[7] The misleading idea was that these potential early adopters would be willing to pay the $1,500 price tag.[8] And having done so, they would encourage the broader consumer segment, everyday consumers with smartphones, to buy the product. But that segment was not asking for a Google Glass at all.

If Google had defined its purpose and identified its main customer audience correctly from the start, things might have gone very differently. To my mind, Google X deliver excellent work, realizing innovative techniques through R&D such as Google Glass or self-driving cars, but unfortunately they undermine their success by failing to run the business properly. Google put its focus too heavily on R&D but forgot the basic commercial premise behind successful innovative products: if they don't work and customers are confused about their purpose, they will not sell.

How to put Principle #1 into practice

Ideation involves creativity, innovation and disruption. Perhaps for that reason it needs to be strongly grounded in the discipline of project management: ideas and options should be subject to rigorous examination to establish their applicability, feasibility and deliverability. Ideation should be framed by good commercial and management practice.

To keep it simple, the first step in every project and any project management methodology should be applying Principle #1: ideation, exploration and experimentation. Here are some tools to use, to get you started.

Design thinking
Design thinking is a method used in ideation and development. It is an approach used to develop solutions that meet the customer's needs and expectations, and to find out what would-be users really need.

The method describes a human-centred, iterative design process consisting of five steps. Design thinking is useful in tackling problems that are ill-defined or unknown. Organizations such as Google and Airbnb have wielded it to notable effect.

Stanford University's Hasso Plattner Institute of Design describes design thinking as having five non-sequential stages.

1 **Empathize:** gain an empathic understanding of the problem you're trying to solve, typically through some form of user research.
2 **Define:** define the core problems you and your team have identified so far.
3 **Ideate:** get ready to start generating ideas. Start to 'think outside the box' to identify new solutions to the problem statement you've created.
4 **Prototype:** produce a number of inexpensive, scaled-down versions of the product so you can investigate the problem solutions generated in the previous stage.
5 **Test:** this is the final stage (however, in an iterative process, the results generated during the testing phase are what you will often use to redefine one or more problems).

Lean Startup

This is a tool to accelerate prototyping and focus on value. Lean Startup is a scientific approach to creating a desired product and getting it into customers' hands faster. Too many projects start with the idea for a product that, in theory, people want. Instead of spending months or years developing a product before taking it to market, Lean will test the assumptions – such as a need for the product, willingness to pay for it, etc. – as early as possible. Lean advocates the creation of a minimum viable product, or MVP, at each stage of development, and testing the market to see if there is traction or interest to pay for your product (or even to get actual paid orders).

These are some of the key benefits of applying Lean Startup concepts in the ideation stages of your project.

1 **Focus on customer problems:** instead of spending time documenting requirements, meet your customer and listen to their problems.
2 **Encourage innovation:** encourage team members to come up with new ideas. Remove the fear of failure.
3 **Shorten delivery cycles:** break up the project into smaller elements, which will allow you to have shorter delivery cycles. Doing so will allow you to identify bottlenecks sooner.
4 **Focus on value:** define what your project's MVP is (i.e. what is actually being asked of the project) and find a solution to deliver that as fast as possible. It can be polished later if the organization has the time and budget. Look for elements of a project that are superficial to the success of the project, and remove them. How many review meetings are needed? How many people should be required for sign-off?

5 Principle #2: A clear purpose informs and inspires

Rationale, (dis)benefits, sustainability

Before embarking on a new project, it is essential to develop a simple purpose statement that articulates both the problem and the solution.

Projects are about change: sometimes that involves building a new piece of infrastructure, or launching a new product, and at other times it is about enabling new behaviour through new software or the launch of a new product. The rationale and business case for a new project will often describe the process of what needs to be done in a form of business or financial language and in a level of granular detail that can, ironically, make the whole thing hard to grasp for the layperson. And if you can't understand what is planned or why, then you're unlikely to be motivated to get involved.

The problem of not being able to see the wood for the trees may be exaggerated for projects where the outcome is intangible, or even uncertain, at the starting point – as is the case for many software or business change projects.

Project success requires that you complement the technical planning documentation by identifying and stating the deeper purpose of the project.

Business case

All project management methodologies require a well-defined business case before projects are ever initiated. By now you probably know that this is never an exact science. Have you ever seen a negative business case?

Business cases are biased. Those responsible for running the project are apt to forget the challenges and shortcomings of earlier projects if they managed ultimately to cross the finishing line. Everyone who pitches a project wants it to be approved, and so they frame their business case on the basis of what they perceive the decision makers want to hear. Decision makers are complicit; how can any project they approve be anything but successful? Consequently, business cases suffer from subjective assumptions about the likely costs, the risks and the ultimate benefits, either through ignorance or deliberate bias. Have you ever seen a project with a negative or meagre return being presented? Optimism bias may lay big projects open to cost or schedule overruns or even to failure. But without it, why would Steve Jobs or any one of those tasked with project approval say 'yes' to the hugely innovative projects for which they are remembered?

Take the example of Concorde, a British–French turbojet-powered supersonic passenger airliner that operated between 1976 and 2003. The business case predicted enormous commercial demand, estimating that up to 350 units would be sold.[1] In the end, cost and restrictions on the routes that could be flown meant that Air France and British Airways were the only airlines to purchase and fly the Concorde. A total of only 20 units were ever built and only 14 of those were sold, representing a £4 billion loss on the project's balance sheet.

Or another ongoing and more recent case: the Hanford nuclear weapons development site in south-eastern Washington state is widely considered to be the most contaminated place in the Western hemisphere. In 1989, the US Energy Department, Environmental Protection Agency and the Washington State Department of Ecology launched an environmental clean-up programme to tackle massive amounts of radioactive and chemical waste. The original plan laid out a thirty-year clean-up programme, but things have not gone according to that plan, and the Hanford clean-up is now expected to take at least seventy years to complete.[2]

There are hundreds of other examples of overly optimistic predictions in high-profile projects. In some cases, this over-optimism is effectively designed into the project from the start, as was the case for the Channel Tunnel project.

A key element of the initial competition in 1994–95 to find a promoter for the Link was the level of direct grants required by each bidder. As the level of direct grants would depend on the amount of revenue each bidder thought it could secure from operating Eurostar UK, there was an in-built incentive for bidders to be over-optimistic about the prospects for the business.[3]

In other words, if you wanted to win the contract, you needed to present (wildly) over-optimistic forecasts. This state of affairs still remains a risk for most government procured projects and programmes today.

Preparation of a business case is a very useful exercise and should not be skipped or cut short. The thinking process, the research, the data gathering and the analysis of the options all help you establish a good, shared understanding of the project and its investment potential. Nevertheless, I recommend caution regarding the business case and the projected returns in financial figures, particularly the expected benefits. Based on my experience, evaluating costs tends to be more accurate than evaluating benefits, where there can be more unknowns, extra assumptions, and the process can extend over years, even decades – assuming the organization bothers to do it at all.

Rationale

To mitigate the risks of an overly optimistic business case, I recommend you think in terms of the rationale for the project.

Viewed simply, the two main rationales for launching a project are either to solve a problem or to seize an opportunity. Ask yourself the following questions before you get started.

- **What is the problem we are going to solve with this project?**
  When the Panama Canal was first built, before the First World War, it was the size of US Navy ships that dictated the width of the locks: 110 feet across and 42 feet deep. The $5 billion upgrade of the canal, opened a hundred years later, was needed to accommodate the modern 'neo-Panamax' ships which can be more than 150 feet wide, extend three football fields in length and have a draught of 50 feet.[4]

- **What is the opportunity we are going to capture with the project?**
  The Airbus A380 was designed to exploit the continued expansion in demand for air travel

(at the time, demand was doubling every fifteen years) while recognizing the challenge of overcrowded landing slots and the need to become more environmentally sustainable.

If the outcome of your planned project cannot easily and plainly be expressed in terms of a problem or an opportunity, then you should refrain from launching your project and research it further until you are confident that you have established the true rationale behind it.

Objectives

In addition to a clear rationale, your project will need at least one SMART objective. The significance of SMART objectives should not be underestimated.

The definition of SMART
These are objectives which are specific, measurable, action-oriented, relevant and time-bound.

- **Specific**
  Plenty of projects have delivered, only to discover that the output isn't what the stakeholders anticipated they would be getting. Your objective needs to distinguish between a project's output and its outcome. For example: 'A solution that enables knowledge storage, publication, discovery and sharing between clients.' Your objective should leave it up to the project team or the developer to decide exactly what solution they will adopt.

- **Measurable**
  In the above example, the measure of success is knowledge storage, publication, discovery and sharing (between clients). If this is happening, then the project is meeting its objectives. In other examples, you may need to provide a specific number target, particularly if the project is designed to improve on a current system or capability.

- **Action-oriented**
  No matter how good your project management skills, an unrealistic strategy or plan will founder. Projects are designed to be stretching (that's the whole point), which means there is always the possibility of failure. But that's not the same as impossible.

- **Relevant**
  In project terms, this translates as resource-based (you need to define how much money or how many resources).

- **Time-bound**
  The schedule is possibly the most challenging aspect of any project. A (very) few projects are temporal (have a fixed end-date) and defined by an event such as a sporting tournament or a corporate acquisition, a regulatory compliance date or an end-of-life date (if something it is replacing is no longer working or no longer available). But *all* projects are subject to time, either because the passage of time may make the output redundant, or because of the ongoing cost of maintaining a project team. That said, arbitrary deadlines (similar to arbitrary budgets) will create unnecessary risk.

Elevator pitch

Every project should have a convincing elevator-pitch statement: something that expresses what it is designed to do in succinct, easily understood and convincing terms. Every business case will include within it a collection of goal statements; fine for testing the credibility of the project at initiation but hardly memorable. How many times have you sat through presentations about new products, software, or business transformation projects without ever being engaged by the idea at the heart of what is being proposed? Your elevator pitch needs to win over hard-hearted commercial directors and, at the same time, act as a clarion call to the people who might work on the project and to the stakeholders who will benefit from it.

All of which doesn't remove from you the responsibility of ensuring that your project rationale and key objective are not being overly optimistic or poorly evidenced. The project manager and sponsor have to ensure that the goals are realistic – or, even better, stretched but achievable.

Purpose

Besides the rationale and a business case, a project should be linked to a higher purpose. Jim Collins and Jerry Porras, authors of the business classic *Built to Last: Successful Habits of Visionary Companies*,[5] provided a useful definition of 'purpose', which we can adapt as follows:

A project's purpose is its fundamental reason for being. An effective purpose reflects the importance people attach to the project's work – it taps their idealistic motivations – and gets at the deeper reasons for a project's existence beyond just making money.

The very word 'purpose' resonates with ideas of identity, values and motivation. It is our value and belief system that sustains us and encourages individuals, teams and societies to achieve extraordinary things; whether these are feats of extraordinary endurance, complex engineering or unimaginable change and transformation.

The most successful project leaders know that by tapping into individuals' hearts as well as their minds, you can inflame their imagination, focus their skills and encourage them to overcome all obstacles and differences to work together. The nice thing about it is that you don't have to be great at something to be passionate about it. Steve Jobs was not the world's greatest engineer, salesperson, designer or businessman. But he was uniquely good enough at all of these things, and was driven by his sense of purpose to do something far greater.

Conversely, too, lack of conviction about a project can quickly be expanded to the rest of the team.

Lessons from Crossrail

The Crossrail Project to deliver the Elizabeth Line, running east-west across the heart of London, is an exercise in complex engineering, complicated supply chains and formidable politics. The project involved building a new railway, with access stations, 40 metres deep and 26 miles long (tunnelled distance) under some of the most valuable real estate in the world, through a tangle of underground train lines, sewers, gas, electricity and communications conduits.

The Crossrail organization's mission statement ('Delivering a world class railway that will fast track the progress of London') and values statement ('Safety, Inspiration, Collaboration, Integrity and Respect') had to sustain the project and unify the large and diverse project team to ensure a safe, high-performing and resilient working environment.

> The core 'client' delivery organisation comprised of 1,200 people from nine different employers, integrated into a single 'Team Crossrail'. Its role was to oversee delivery from 20 principal contractors, each with their own supply chain – a peak workforce of 14,000. This diverse team ranged from technical office roles to site construction roles, geographically dispersed across more than 40 separate projects. Some of the principal contractors operated in a joint venture environment and brought vision, mission and values from their home organisations. Taking into account that the staff of some contractors also had limited access to technology because of the nature of their role, developing and rolling out a common vision, mission and values was challenging.[6]

How to put Principle #2 into practice

Psychologists have done extensive research on the impact positive thinking and 'believing in success' can have on individuals. In fact, success is a self-fulfilling prophecy. When we expect to succeed, we automatically mobilize our internal resources to achieve the expected, and all this happens without our rational consent. Moreover, when others believe in us, the dynamic is reinforced. That is why it is important for a project leader to create a positive environment where successes are applauded and the difficulties of a project are downplayed, so that a can-do spirit and attitude are cultivated in the team. People need someone who believes in them so they can believe in themselves.

Clarity of both the purpose and the ultimate benefits of a project are fundamental, not just to ensure a coherent investment decision-making process but to guide and motivate the project team throughout the whole endeavour. Ask yourself the following questions.

- Does everyone involved in or affected by the project understand what you are planning to do and why? (They may understand the project from their own perspective, and that's fine, but all of these perspectives need to complement each other.)
- How is your rationale expressed? Do you have a workable statement for expressing what the project will achieve, and is it clear what problem or opportunity this is addressing?
- Does your rationale allow you not simply to express success but also to identify if and when your project exceeds its scope? Or when you start to diverge from the original vision through poor procurement or poor project practice?

Once your project is under way, it is very easy to lose sight of the original intent in the pressure of managing a complex project. Ideation allows you to identify the best possible (or best feasible) solution for your project. If you have taken the time to discuss and explore alternative solutions, you will already have a sense of what won't work or what is suboptimal, so this early preparation time not only helps assure a great project rationale but will help with managing the project too.

Principle #2 highlights the importance of a clear purpose that informs and inspires. Here are some tools to use, to get you started.

Choose the purpose

Your project's purpose is its north star. Defining your project's purpose is all about clarity and alignment. The purpose should not simply be fancy words – it has to be genuine and it has to feel meaningful.

Simon Sinek highlights the common practice in most organizations of setting essentially meaningless objectives: 'I live in a world in which the overwhelming pressure is to make the numbers, hit the target . . . it's all very finite . . . most people are incentivized based on "if you hit your numbers by a certain date". Neglecting the facts that both those numbers and those dates are arbitrary.'[7]

These are a few questions that can help you to determine the purpose of your project.

- Why does the project matter?
- What opportunity would be lost if the project were not carried out?
- To whom does the project matter most? The sponsor, the project leader, everyone?
- Why would anyone dedicate their precious time, energy and passion to the project?

Another easier method of identifying the purpose of a project is to ask, 'Why are you doing the project?' In many cases you'll need to repeat the question. Usually, it is necessary to ask this question five to seven times. Use the 'why' question in response to each of the answers you receive, to get to the essence of the matter. Once you have the real reason, substitute the original 'why' with 'by when' and 'how much'. If after the exercise you still have not reached something concrete, then I would strongly recommend that you rethink and do not start the whole project.

Here are some questions to check the appeal of the project's purpose, and to help you identify a project's passion.

- Does the project have an emotional element?
- How does the project make you (and those around you) feel?
- What makes the project great and unique?
- What will be remembered about the project ten or twenty years from now?
- Why would anyone want to be part of the project team? What aspects would make people volunteer to participate and to contribute to the project?
- Do the values associated with the project and its 'kerb appeal' align with its purpose? Is the project's passion aligned with the project's purpose?

Develop and share stories

This is an effective tool to engage the organization. Strategy implementation guru Jeroen De Flander explained to me, 'Stories make messages stickier. Wrap a story around your message and it becomes twenty times easier for the listener to remember.'[8] Stories put information in a context that people can relate to.

They also offer a second benefit, which is to facilitate an emotional connection – they 'reach for the heart'. And the great thing about stories, including project stories, is that they do not have to be invented, just spotted. As Anders Indset, a world-leading business philosopher, pointed out to me, 'Jeff Bezos is not using PowerPoints, he's using storytelling, and people are tapping into that, getting an understanding of the topics, trying to visualize how to explain it. And that's how a project succeeds, and I'm a strong believer in that.'[9]

Use SMART objectives

Define objectives that will stick in people's minds. Since they were first introduced by George T. Doran in 1981,[10] SMART objectives have become an essential tool to focus people on what really matters and remove distractions. Every successful project needs at least one clearly articulated objective. As we saw earlier in this chapter, SMART is an acronym for the following five elements.

- **S**pecific: provide the 'who' and the 'what' of the project.
- **M**easurable: focus on 'how much' the project will produce.
- **A**ction-oriented: trigger practical actions to achieve the project objective.
- **R**elevant: accurately address the purpose of the project.
- **T**ime-bound: have a time frame indicating when the objective will be met.

The project to deliver the London Olympics in 2012 is a great example of SMART objectives in action. The project's mission was: 'To deliver venues, facilities, infrastructure and transport for the London 2012 Olympic and Paralympic Games on time, to budget and to leave a lasting legacy.' The objectives were clearly set out.

- To create infrastructure and facilities associated with Games' venues to time and agreed budget in accordance with the principles of sustainable development.
- To deliver Olympic and Paralympic venues to time, to design and building specification, and to agreed budget, providing for agreed legacy use.
- To deliver the necessary transport infrastructure for the Games, and devise and implement effective transport plans which provide for legacy use.
- To assist the LDA in the finalization of sustainable legacy plans for the Park and all venues.

Everyone involved in the team working on the Olympics was very clear on what needed to be done, by whom and by when. The result was a project that delivered the infrastructure, on time and on budget, which then enabled a hugely successful Games.

6 Principle #3: The sponsor is both advocate and accountable

Advocate, godparent, executive

The governance of the project, and the allocation of accountability and responsibility, is a key area to secure in the early stages of the project. Just as an organization or business has a chief executive, who is in charge and accountable for its operations, the same is true for a project, where the executive sponsor is accountable for the overall success or failure of the project. Establishing a clear governance structure at the beginning of the initiative is essential, as is selecting a sponsor with the requisite skill set that qualifies them to lead the project to success.

The measure of success for which the sponsor is accountable is the *benefit(s)* that will accrue once the project has delivered, or is being operated or exploited by the users (clients, employees and citizens). This is significant because it means that the sponsor not only needs to make sure that the project delivers but also that the benefits associated with the project are still desirable and achievable. This explains why they have to be an advocate. This involves sense-checking throughout the project that it is still needed or, in the event that things have changed, redirecting or recommending the project's cancellation if continued advocacy is no longer appropriate. Note that today there is pressure to deliver benefits before the project is fully delivered, requiring more agile ways to look at how the project will be structured.

Many projects still start without any clear decision being taken about who is ultimately accountable for their successful delivery. As projects tend to run across geographies, business units, functions, departments and organizational boundaries, they are often prone to 'shared accountability and collective sponsorship'. As a result, many executives feel responsible, yet no one is really accountable for driving the project to completion.

Once, when I was speaking to the CEO of a large global telecoms company, he bluntly admitted that, 'Currently, I am the executive sponsor of eighteen projects. The three projects to which I dedicate time to follow through – by supporting the project leader and team, and chairing the steering committee – go much better than the fifteen that I sponsor but to which I really don't dedicate any time.'

Organizations need to understand that the executive sponsor is one of the most vital and influential roles in any project, especially in those projects that are strategic and transversal (across departments, organizations or supply chains). The more complex the project, the more critical the executive sponsor role and the more time it demands.[1]

The importance of active steering

The executive sponsor, together with the project manager, sets the tone for the project and defines the project governance. Governance involves a definition of the various contributing roles, stakeholders and decision-making bodies for the project. Once the areas of responsibility are clearly defined, they are represented by a project organizational chart.

One of the most important bodies in a project is the steering committee, which is chaired by the executive sponsor and run by the project manager. The members and the frequency with which they meet often determine the importance the project has for the organization.

I remember being on a large integration project of two European banks. Its steering committee, chaired by the CEO, met every day at 5 p.m. to discuss the status of the merger. Imagine the pressure that this imposed on the organization. For all of us, it was evident that the integration project was the number-one priority, and we had to show progress every day. In contrast, I have also worked on a project where the steering committee met every three months. To make matters worse, most senior leaders didn't show up because they had other priorities, and those who were present barely remembered what the project was about.

Unsurprisingly, the first project was extremely successful, the second a complete failure.

What does an absence of effective sponsorship look like?

In 2004, the UK's Department for Communities and Local Government launched a project called FiReControl, which aimed to improve the resilience, efficiency and technology of the Fire and Rescue Service.

In 2010, having already spent £245 million, it was estimated that the final spend required to deliver the project could be as much as £635 million (more than five times the total original budget) and the project was cancelled. The UK National Audit Office highlighted the failings of accountability and governance that had contributed to such poor project performance:

'Governance arrangements in the first five years of the project were complex and ineffective, which led to unclear lines of responsibility and slow decision-making.'[2]

Without strong governance, the inertia of the organization will make a project battle for resources and attention, leading the project to delays and eventually to failure.

To address these organizational forces, senior leaders need to play a key role in supporting the project and providing the resources and time required to complete the work. Therefore, it is essential for the success of large transversal projects that senior leaders assume the steering committee roles and responsibilities reflected in the project organizational chart.

The benefit of clear governance

Here are three of the organizational challenges faced by projects, which executives need to be aware of and which strong governance will address.

- **Resources are often not fully dedicated to the project, and people have other responsibilities.**
  For example, a Java development expert whose main job is to keep the website up and running is asked to join a digitization project. Her current responsibilities are not modified, therefore her contribution to the strategic project will be on top of her day-to-day job. Not being fully dedicated will have an impact on the speed of the project.

- **Resources have different reporting lines outside the project.**

For example, a legal expert is part of a GDPR (General Data Protection Regulation) project, which is led by the vice president of the business. The legal expert is not participating in the weekly project team meetings. The vice president has tried to convince the legal expert to join, but as she doesn't report to him she doesn't feel obliged to follow his instructions.

- **Departments' objectives are different and regularly more important than the project's objectives.**
  For example, a finance controller is required to participate in the development of the business case of a large company-wide project. However, his direct boss, the CFO, is under pressure to finalize the annual accounts, a key objective for the finance department. Despite having some tight deadlines, the project is at the mercy of the CFO's willingness to cooperate.

Shortly after Fortis Bank collapsed in 2008 with the financial crisis, BNP Paribas made an offer to the Belgian Government to acquire the distressed bank. In May 2009 the acquisition was approved by the shareholders. Baudouin Prot, CEO of BNP Paribas, announced: 'The project of tying up with Fortis Bank will be strongly value creative for all stakeholders.' And to lead the integration project he appointed BNP Paribas CFO, Jean-Laurent Bonnafé, who was sent to Brussels on a clear mission: Fortis had to be integrated within the next three years. He established a daily steering committee, which included all the business and function heads, where they reviewed closely the status of the integration. The pressure on the organization was tremendous. The entire 15,000-strong workforce was in no doubt about what their priority was, and where they had to spend their time: integration activities.

Jean-Laurent Bonnafé played an extremely active role in the project; he was what I call an engaged, committed and decisive sponsor. Needless to say, the integration project was a success, completed one year in advance of the stated deadline.

How to put Principle #3 into practice

Principle #3 highlights the importance of selecting a sponsor with the necessary level of belief and skills, who will oversee and drive the project, in addition to providing sufficient time and focus. Here are some tools to use, to get you started.

Select the right executive sponsor

Most of the time, the executive sponsor is naturally selected, based on where the project originates. However, here are a few criteria that may help you to choose the right person.

- Who has the highest vested interest in the outcome of the project?
- Are they the owner of a budget, both financial and in terms of resources?
- Are they high enough up in the organization to be able to make budget decisions?
- Are they ready to dedicate at least one day of their time each week to support the project?
- (Preferably) do they have a good understanding of the technical matters of the project?

- Are they clearly accountable for the outcome of the project? Do they understand their obligations and responsibility?
- Will they demonstrate through their approach that the project for which they have oversight is a priority alongside their other work?

Clarify the responsibilities of the executive sponsor
Sponsors have oversight of the project in three areas.

- **The financial aspects of the project** – the budget and costs.

  Making sure that the project is running to schedule and on budget, overseeing changes to either (if required) and assuring the business case.

- **The way that the project is run** – that it is managed both ethically and in line with the requirements of the business.

  Projects are collaborative enterprises, often involving individuals and organizations beyond the client company or project owner. The project sponsor is guardian of the trust associated with that collaboration.

- **The benefits that the project is designed to deliver** – perhaps the most challenging element.

  Specifically, sense-checking the project at regular intervals to make sure that it will continue to deliver the benefits that were agreed during the planning stages, and eventually accelerate them. The project sponsor has the power to redirect, pause or even advocate closure if, for any of these reasons, the project starts to drift.

As a minimum, the following points summarize the responsibilities of the executive sponsor. They will:

- ensure the project's strategic significance – which means they need to understand both the project and the organization's strategy
- establish approval and funding for the project – remember, the idea is not to establish approval at all costs, so the sponsor needs to ensure the business case is realistic
- achieve (or ensure) support from key stakeholders – as a senior manager within the organization, the sponsor has influence and should use it
- resolve conflicts and make decisions – when issues are escalated up to the sponsor, it is important that they are willing to take responsibility for their solution
- be accessible and approachable – on-call support for the project leader (the project sponsor is one of the roles that reflects the model of the 'leader as facilitator')
- participate in periodic reviews – having the requisite time to prepare for and attend reviews should be a key part of the sponsor's personal performance measures
- chair the steering committee – playing the role of honest broker
- encourage recognition – project teams that succeed are often undervalued because the essence of good project management is avoiding drama and crisis
- support closure review – the two elements of many closure reviews (lessons learned and benefits realization assessment) are among the most overlooked, and yet they underpin organizational performance and development

- be ultimately accountable for the project – the project sponsor needs to have 'skin in the game' (if they don't believe the project will deliver the benefits that were originally agreed, then it's their job to redirect the project, require changes or recommend cancellation).

Use the Responsibility Assignment Matrix (RACI)

The RACI (Responsible, Accountable, Consulted, Informed) matrix is a very useful tool for cross-matching key activities with the various roles in a project.[3] If you understand the difference between those who are responsible for delivering a change process (usually the project team) and those who are ultimately accountable for it (the decision makers) and between those who need to be consulted before any decisions are made and those who simply wish to be kept abreast of developments, then you will have a good basis for allocating the work and planning your communications.

Use the matrix to reflect who does what. It considers who should be:

- **R**esponsible (for carrying out the activity)
- **A**ccountable (the ultimate owner of the activity)
- **C**onsulted (individuals or groups that need to be consulted and provide input), and
- **I**nformed (individuals or groups that ought to be informed).

7 Principle #4: Customer needs drive the solution

Voice of the customer; definition, design and scope; requirements and boundaries

As in so many aspects of business and government, customers are at the heart of successful projects. In this case, customers can mean commercial customers, but also might mean internal customers, citizens and users of the project's results and benefits at large.

Phil Driver summarizes what organizations do in the following terms: 'Organizations create assets (products, services and infrastructure) and enable customers and citizens to use these assets to create benefits (outcomes) for themselves and others.'[1]

If customers and citizens (the users in Phil's definition) are the ones who realize the benefits of a project, it follows that unless your project is driven by their needs, it is on a hiding to nothing. How many IT projects have failed because the users simply ignore the new system?

Understanding and agreeing what the project will consist of and deliver is one of the *raisons d'être* of project management. Different organizations use different terms to describe this (for example, scope, or specifications, detailed requirements, design and functionality). The scope is the most important element in making an accurate estimation of the cost, duration, plan and benefits of the project.

Depending on the type of project, defining the scope in the early stages may range from the straightforward to the impossible and anything in between. Projects that deliver tangible outcomes, using existing construction or engineering, may be relatively straightforward; although even this may be subject to change, particularly if the project is looking forward some time into the future There are other projects, however, in which the scope will be impossible to determine at the beginning (for example, a digital transformation initiative). Therefore, duration and costs estimated at the beginning of the project will be largely inaccurate, sometimes by a factor of five or more. Basically, if the project only has a vague scope, the time and cost estimated on that basis will be utterly wrong.

The defence dilemma

Between 1997 and 2009, the UK Ministry of Defence was heavily criticized for its approach to commissioning new armoured vehicles. Over that period, it only managed to deliver two out of the eight new vehicle projects it commissioned. Indeed, between 1998 and 2010 it managed to spend £1.1 billion without delivering its principal armoured vehicles. The ministry struggled to develop an approach to designing a project scope that was able to reflect the fact that, rather than commissioning the vehicles of today, they needed to commission vehicles for the future.

> Complex requirements have been set which rely on technological advances to achieve a qualitative advantage over the most demanding potential adversaries. However, for vehicles procured using the standard acquisition process there has not been an effective means to assess the costs, risks and amount of equipment needed to meet

these requirements in the early stages. These demanding requirements often reduce the scope to maximise competition which in turn can lead to cost increases, delays to the introduction of equipment into service and reductions to the numbers of vehicles bought to stay within budgets.[2]

The other common challenge is that even if the scope has been well defined at the beginning of the project, there is a good chance that it will change during the life cycle of the project (also known as 'scope creep'). This will again impact the duration, cost, plans and benefits of the project. The more the scope changes (i.e. in terms of design, requirements, functionality, features and characteristics), the more challenging it is to deliver the project successfully and according to the initial plan.

The clue should be in the name

The purchase of 60 buses at a cost of nearly $750,000 for the Nelson Mandela Bay Metropolitan Municipality in South Africa in 2009 was part of a project to create what the project called 'an Integrated Public Transport System'.

Unfortunately, problems with the scope and the design of the system resulted in bus lanes that were impractical, zebra crossings that obstructed traffic flow, and design flaws that represented a danger to users of the system. The buses themselves were too large for the roadway and were delivered with the access doors on the wrong side. Following a short period during the 2010 South African World Cup, the buses have been parked up and never used.[3]

Inadequate consultation, poor requirements planning and a scope that was clearly unfit for purpose have resulted in a system that could not be less integrated if you tried.

Moving a national icon

The development of a new Broadcasting Centre for the BBC was always going to be challenging. Contractors faced complex challenges during the construction phase due to the site location in a busy, residential and constricted area; the underground tube lines; and the Grade II listed status of the building.

The original Art Deco Broadcasting House was designed by George Val Myer. The building has nine floors above the ground and three floors below. With Portland stone surface, the façade and foyer are designed with sculptures carved by Eric Gill. The structure was extended in 1961 and 1995.

The redeveloped Broadcasting House has three buildings linked together around a public courtyard. The new extension building is a 10-floor structure with three basement levels. The curved entrance of the extended building has a glass front and the roof is of a gull-wing shape. It used similar materials to those of the existing building such as Portland stone and glass-cladding. A Jaume Plensa memorial sculpture is installed on the rooftop.

The curved façade and neighbouring buildings have been designed with a night-time lighting scheme. It creates a unified composition with the neighbouring buildings such as John Nash's All Souls Church. Public spaces for the staff are arranged at the central part of the complex with walkways, break-out areas, education and exhibition spaces, shops, food outlets and a theatre.[4]

The National Audit Office verdict on the project highlighted the shortcomings of the initial scope.

Phase 1 of the Broadcasting House project ran into serious difficulties. It is a complex project with significant risks, but the full scope of the project was not defined clearly at the outset, and weak governance and poor change control processes contributed to severe delays and increased costs. In 2004, the BBC improved the governance of the project, making significant changes to the management of the remaining stages, and the BBC Governors commissioned consultants to conduct a review of these changes in 2006.[5]

The BBC story highlights the importance of correctly iden-tifying the customer need before you start, and building an accurate set of requirements and a project scope to match. Get these initial elements wrong and you are likely to strug-gle with change and governance. And it's also likely to impact your contractors, which will increase the costs and lengthen the schedule, if it doesn't also introduce the risk of contract disputes.

How to put Principle #4 into practice

At the beginning of the project, gather the main stakeholders and key contributors together to define and agree to the scope, in as detailed a manner as possible. Don't be afraid of taking some extra days to address major uncertainties. A delay of one week during the scoping phase can save significant time later. If the uncertainty leads to a change during the implementation, it will probably lead to a longer delay, and perhaps derail the whole project.

'I don't want to build a game, I want to build a universe.' Chris Roberts is the driving force behind *Star Citizen*, a crowd-funded, multiplayer, online game. The scale of the project is breathtaking, with nearly $200 million in funding. This is the ultimate project, developed on the basis of customer needs.

The project has two million backers – essentially the future customers. Pledging to the project is voluntary and there are no legal obligations for the backers, which means the project team need to do as much as they can to make the audience happy; using weekly release reports on work done, show casts, beta-versions for their customers to try.

Most projects don't have that level of intimate connection between investors and customers, nor would they want to, but any project could learn from the engagement activity, which serves to build the user base and to validate the work that is being done.[6]

Principle #4 highlights the importance of putting your customers front and centre of the project and how you manage it. Here are some tools to use, to get you started.

Use the BOSCARD method

This was created in the 1980s by Cap Gemini to help define the scope and requirements of projects. The BOSCARD framework allows you to frame the project in a way that is transparent to all and to set the parameters for 'who does what and why'. The framework consists of the following seven questions.

1 **Background – what is the background of the project?**
   Describe the relevant facts to show an understanding
   of the environment, political, business and other
   contexts in which the project will be carried out.

2 **Objective – what are the key objectives?**
   State the goals of the project and demonstrate an
   understanding of its business rationale (the 'why').

3 **Scope – what is the solution the project will implement?**
   Describe what the project will develop and break
   its various stages down into milestones. Describe
   the resources that will be made available and the
   corresponding external partners, if applicable.

4 **Constraints – what are the key constraints to deliver
   the project successfully?**
   Describe the key challenges and blocking factors to
   be addressed in planning the project.

5 **Assumptions – what are the main assumptions made?**
   State the key hypothesis that has been used to define
   the project rationale, objectives, plan and budget.
   If assumptions change later, it might justify a
   renegotiation of the project.

6 **Risks – what are the risks that could make the
   project fail?**
   List the risks that may materialize and affect the
   realization of the objectives of the project. Also, list
   any risks that could have an impact on the timeline
   and finances (such as tax and other transaction costs).

7 **Deliverables – what are the desired outcomes of the project?**
Describe the key elements that will be produced by the project, and how they connect to each other and to the project objectives.

By addressing each area, you can be clear on what is expected to be done and not done, and have an upfront discussion on the boundaries of the project with the executive sponsor and key stakeholders.

Employ user-centred design

This is a concept that introduces agile methods for defining and building the project scope. It has grown out of the software development industry and has now become established as a means of understanding customer needs and placing them at the heart of how a project is run and the shape of the product, service, building or (increasingly) government policy.

The key element in many such cases is the user journey (or the patient or citizen experience), which describes the timeline for the customer's interaction with whatever is the output of the project, along with the decisions the customer makes on the way, the experiences the customer has and the outcome of the interaction.

The reason why user-centred design is so important to projects is because many depend on user behaviour to achieve the benefits and their commercial aims. Let's take the German Energiewende as an example (see Chapter 3). Ultimately the project is designed to change the way German citizens (and, by extension, citizens in the wider world) perceive and consume energy.

For some projects, particularly those associated with

technology – which, increasingly, is the majority of projects for the consumer – the pace of change adds a considerable element of complexity to the design. The designers and then those delivering the project are working with emerging technology for which consumer behaviour may not yet be fully understood.

One design agency describes the user experience associated with a new challenger bank (challenger banks in the UK are new, startup consumer banking services that 'challenge' the handful of established and monolithic banks that control 90 per cent of the market) in their blog.[7]

If we are talking about digital banking disruption in the near future, how will it work? I believe, challenger banks, as a delightful banking customer experience providers, will be based on 10 emerging digital banking trends that you may already know.

1   Blockchain
2   Gamification
3   Nudge theory
4   Robo advising
5   Voice processing
6   Biometrics
7   Social integration
8   Personalization
9   Big data
10 Open API and clouds

Running a project to establish a new challenger banking service therefore requires the project team to understand how customers will interact with some technologies of which the customer is as yet still unaware.

8 Principle #5: Realistic planning involves both ambition and pragmatism

Process, milestones, resources, cost

The essence of Principle #5 is the need to temper your ambition with a realistic assessment of the required and available resources, time and people. Project management enables you to deliver things (for example, products, software, buildings, processes and systems) but it doesn't change the immutable laws of nature. You can only work on as many projects as you have time, money and people for. So it's very important that you 'cut your coat according to your cloth'.

Project planning

'Time is money.' This famous phrase, attributed to Benjamin Franklin, is an absolute when planning projects. Time is one of the major characteristics of projects: unless there is an articulated, compelling, official and publicly announced deadline, there is a good chance that the project will be delivered later than originally planned. Delays in projects have a twofold impact: they involve additional, unplanned costs (if nothing else, simply the overhead of running a project team for longer than anticipated), but they also involve a loss of benefits and expected returns, both having a tremendous negative impact on the business case of the initiative. A project without a deadline should not be considered a project – better to call it an experiment, an exploration, or daily business activities.

Lost passenger journeys mean lost revenue

When the delay to the launch of one of London's flagship projects, the Crossrail link that runs underneath the city from east to west, was announced at the end of 2018, an immediate casualty was the new owners for whom the line was being built.

Transport for London (TfL) is the body responsible for London underground and bus services. When they took on Crossrail, they were already anticipating the revenues it would generate for them at the scheduled end of the project, in July 2018.

The delay to the launch, announced shortly after that, was estimated to cost TfL £600 million in lost fares. The final figure is likely to be considerably higher as the delay continues. This shortfall has been exacerbated by the decision of London's mayor earlier in 2018 to freeze tube fares for the benefit of hard-pressed travellers.

The power of deadlines

Olympic Games, World Cups and World Expositions are massive projects that have fixed deadlines, announced and established years in advance. The way these projects are implemented varies significantly according to the means available and the country's working culture: some are finished years in advance (Beijing 2008), others just in time (Athens 2004 or Rio de Janeiro 2016). However, what is extraordinary is that, despite all the challenges and different ways of dealing with projects, so far the Olympic Games have always delivered on time!

Time, and deadlines, are essential to help people focus and to exert some pressure on getting the work done.

One of the best examples of the immense power of deadlines is the project of landing the first man on the moon. When he announced his bold dream, in May 1961, US President John F. Kennedy set a clear deadline: 'By the end of the 1960s.' That deadline stuck in people's minds, and it pushed them to work together to achieve an impossible dream. That deadline was one of the project's biggest success factors. Without that deadline, it is uncertain when (if ever) humans would have landed on the moon. The bill for the 1969 moon landing by the Apollo 11 lunar module came to $25.4 billion;[1] it remains one of the most expensive projects in history, yet one of humanity's greatest accomplishments.

Time in projects behaves in peculiar ways. A week at the beginning of a project is no longer and no shorter than a week at the end of the project, but it just doesn't feel the same. The closer to the deadline, the more nervous people will become and the greater the tendency to make mistakes. In many ways, the role of the project leader is similar to the role of the conductor of an orchestra. They set the tempo and intermediary deadlines, which vary throughout the project life cycle.

The power of ambition

Some of the most recognized international airlines are now based in the Persian Gulf and have experienced an exceptional increase in operations in the past few years. There are two main reasons behind their success.

- They were founded by the rich governments of those countries to which they belong, and have enjoyed sustained access to further investment ever since.
- Their natural area of operations included routes largely ignored until then by other flag carriers.

This enabled Emirates, Etihad Airways and Qatar Airways to develop an alternative and successful business model, based on a hub-and-spoke approach, which ultimately provides a large number of operations from a 'hub airport' that allows multiple connections between flights originating from and destined for key international centres.

At the point when this business model no longer supported further expansion, these airlines had to innovate to keep growing. This is the origin of the ambitious acquisition and partnering programmes that these companies developed to target other airlines in markets in which they did not already operate. In 2011 Etihad disclosed a major programme to acquire a stake in several smaller airlines, based in various geographical areas, as a means of building a network of flights centred on Etihad's main airport base and home city: Abu Dhabi. Since then, Etihad has bought shares in companies such as Air Berlin (29 per cent), Alitalia (49 per cent), Jet Airways (24 per cent) and Virgin Australia (21 per cent). The common denominator of all these companies is that, at the point of their acquisition by Etihad, they were struggling to survive.

A movie that was all about schedule

Richard Linklater's movie *Boyhood* took twelve years from the start of filming to the final public release. The schedule was entirely intentional, because the director wanted to display the evolution and growth of a young boy, Mason, and of his family, through Mason's own eyes. The film-maker used the emerging platform of social media to sustain public interest in the project throughout its long gestation.

At the start of the project, Linklater had a plan for the final scene, as well as ideas for what he would shoot on the way there, but the intervening scenes were planned prior to each year's shooting. This made the movie a global project, consisting of a series of scenes planned and shot every year and then edited together to create a unique movie which made the viewers reflect on their childhood and personal growth by presenting them with a realistic scenario that they could have lived. The ageing of the actors meant that, as with many projects, there was no opportunity to reshoot scenes from earlier years should the director find gaps in the story during the edit.[2]

Many large projects share human characteristics with *Boyhood*. The stakeholders develop, their aspirations and plans are likely to grow with the project, and the context and external environment change too, making it difficult to rework parts of the project if they fail to keep up with these changing perspectives.

Project costs and investment

The budget in any project is largely composed of the time spent by the resources dedicated to all the phases of the project. Resources include the people working on the project plus all other investments (consultants, material, software, hardware, etc.) required to develop the scope of the project. The budget is, together with time and scope, the third main constraint in traditional project management. Without a budget, there is no project, and the accuracy of the budget estimates depends on the scope's definition and its stability.

In the yearly budgeting and resource allocation cycle, organizations usually have two main types of budgets: capital and operational.

- The **capital** expenditure (often called CAPEX) budget is fully allocated to large investment projects, which makes the execution of projects easier.
- The **operational** expenditure (often called OPEX) budget is often larger than CAPEX and is used for the resources that are running the organization.

Two of the most frequently encountered challenges for organizations are the ambiguity between projects that are funded from the OPEX budget, and the allocation of resources between operations and project activities. However you budget, dedicating sufficient resources to a project is critical for ensuring its success.

The luxury of an unlimited budget

Some extraordinary projects enjoy an unlimited budget. This helps to engage more resources, accelerate the project and deliver it successfully. This is often the case for projects that are launched and supported by senior leaders or top officials, such as some of the majestic projects built in the Middle East in the past decade. For example, the Burj Khalifa – at 828 metres the tallest building in the world – was sponsored by the ruler of Dubai. The project didn't have any problems with budget. Construction began in 2004, with the exterior completed five years later, and the building opened to the public in 2010.

However, having an unlimited budget is no guarantee of success. If some of the key elements described in this chapter are missing, there are chances that the project will fail.

The benefits of a portfolio process

Planning the schedule for the most important and strategic projects needs to be done as part of a portfolio process. The executive team need to prioritize which of the projects are most important and which are most urgent, and the portfolio team need to balance this against the resources available. This doesn't necessarily mean that all of the most important projects are first in the queue. Portfolio management will also take into account dependencies between different projects, the amount of investment funding available, the people and other resources available, and the relative risk of different projects. The idea is to smooth the flow of projects, match aspirations to resources, and give every project at least an even chance of meeting its schedule.

We all have a natural bias towards wanting to start things we have agreed on, so one of the big challenges for any portfolio team is to check and challenge any end-dates that are unnecessarily early.

How to put Principle #5 into practice

The budget is derived directly from the scope of the project and the urgency to deliver. The more detailed the scope and the more fixed it is, the more accurately the budget will be estimated. To reduce the risk of budget overruns, never allocate the total amount of the budget to the project at the beginning. Break it down into portions. Establish quarterly review cycles to check status and budget consumption. If the project's original business case is still valid, release another portion of budget. If the project is having major problems, ignore sunk costs and seriously consider cancelling it.

Principle #5 highlights the importance of tempering ambition with realism. Here are some tools to use, to get you started.

Define your project plan using top-down, bottom-up estimation

The best and most accurate way to create a plan and establish a realistic deadline is to start with an initial high-level (top-down) orientation to agree the best timing to complete the project (for example, a launch date or opening day). Once you have broken down the project scope into activities, review them all from the bottom up, to check whether the initial deadline is realistic. If not, you'll need to think of ways of reducing the duration of the project: for example, by adding resources, by working in parallel or by delivering the project in discrete phases. Where possible, reducing the deadline by between 5 and 20 per cent will encourage the team to innovate and focus on key deliverables.

Working with intermediary deadlines (or milestones) of about three to six weeks (depending on the overall timescale) will help you to maintain the momentum. With anything beyond that, there is a risk that people will hesitate and may procrastinate until they are close to the milestone date, at which stage they then panic and rush, with the risk of impacting the final quality of the project.

Adopt an agile approach to progress

Many projects, whatever the methodology used to deliver them, may present the opportunity for a series of scaled releases. Finishing parts of the project and releasing them for customers to use can help reduce schedule pressures. Agile project management is a methodology that was initially developed in the software industry for precisely this kind of reason and because of its value in enabling customers to familiarize themselves with and validate the work as it was being done. It is particularly useful when the outcome of the project you are working on is not necessarily defined in absolute terms.

Taking an agile approach allows you to progress step-by-step, as opposed to more traditional methods where a project, once launched, may be very hard to recover if it starts to drift from the original schedule.

Define your project cost and budget using top-down, bottom-up estimation

It is important to note that most of the cost in a project is the time spent by the team members (human resources) to perform the project activities. The best and most accurate way to create a budget is by first having an initial high-level (top-down) orientation on the total project cost. Identify the potential budget available and look at the costs of similar past projects. Then, after breaking the project scope down into activities, estimate the cost of each activity (bottom up).

As with the planning, this exercise should be carried out together with the main contributors to the project. Some activities will be performed by external parties who need to provide their cost projections. There will be some activities and additional costs associated with integrating the project into the regular 'business-as-usual' activities of whoever is using whatever the project has created. Adding together the costs of all the activities will provide an accurate view of the total investment required to carry out the project. Large projects usually include a contingency amount (5–10 per cent) of the total estimated cost to handle unforeseen expenses. Compare the bottom-up estimate with the initial top-down estimate and see whether there is a big gap. If that is the case, and there is an important budget constraint, consider reducing the scope or even re-evaluating carrying out the project.

In the case of some projects, you may know the direction in which you are trying to go without being able to articulate the scope completely because the project itself will help define the final outcome. Where that is the case, it makes sense to set an initial development budget and then re-budget (redirect or reframe the project) once your early work has enabled you to establish what you are trying to do.

9 Principle #6: The perfect is the enemy of the good

Test, assure, excel

Principle #6 encourages you to keep the purpose and the customer in mind, whenever you are managing a project. Use your imagination to progress a step at a time towards a successful outcome, keeping your eye on what that is at all times.

Ensuring that the outcome of the project meets the quality expectations and the customer requirements is an integral part of project management, yet it is often overlooked or not a priority. Teams frequently focus on doing the work and leave the quality part to the end of the project, when adjustments are most expensive.

Recognizing when you are no longer progressing

The launch of a new state-of-the-art airport in Denver was delayed for 16 months by shortcomings in the highly innovative automated baggage handling facility, costing the airport $560 million. This was compounded by the finished system, which carried maintenance costs of $1 million a month.[1]

Compare this with the development of the new automated baggage handling facility at Heathrow Airport's Terminal 3. The project involved a complete rethink of how baggage is prepared and delivered to the aircraft, and the state-of-the-art centre needed to be built in the middle of one of the busiest working airports in the world, involving multiple contractors, multiple elements and a major change management programme for the handlers themselves.

The success of the project was put down to the decision to create an integrated project team of Heathrow staff and contractors who 'started the project with the end in mind'.[2]

It is the responsibility of the project manager to ensure that a project meets, or exceeds, the expected quality. Any project for which the outcome becomes unfit for purpose needs to be cancelled.

Quality validation is key

Some projects require official and significant quality-validation tests in order to start commercial production. This is the case with many infrastructure, production, life science and engineering projects.

Refurbishment brings its own quality requirements

Building validation involves several distinct assessments.[3] A condition report is required for buildings that are being repurposed or reused. Similarly, there is a need to assure the space is compliant with the people and systems that will be occupying it: does the building have the requisite capacity, not just in terms of physical space but in terms of the heating and cooling or other systems? Risk management will look at issues such as maintenance (which was such a problem for the Denver Airport project).

The role of user testing and simulations

For IT development, it is common to do user testing and other simulations to ensure that the end product satisfies the needs of the organization. Traditionally, the testing of new systems has been done towards the end of the project, often leading to additional work and delays in the schedule. Nowadays, with agile development methods, quality checks are often done on a weekly basis.

One of Apple's greatest strengths is that it makes its products look and feel easy to use. But there was nothing easy about making the iPhone – its inventors say the process was often nerve-wracking. Steve Jobs wanted to see a demo of everything. Designers would often create mock-ups of a single design element – such as a button on the iPhone – up to fifty times, until it met his stellar quality standards.[4]

Ensuring quality and consistency

Think about the Summer Olympic Games, which take place every four years and are the most watched event in the world. Quality and consistency are paramount for the event organizers. The most recent summer Games, held in Rio de Janeiro in 2016, drew in an audience of 3.6 billion viewers. Every event, every venue, every image has to meet the highest standards, no matter where the event takes place.

The selection of the host city is made by the International Olympic Committee (IOC) seven years before those particular Games are scheduled to be held. Apart from the host city and country, the format is pretty much the same: 16 days' duration, approximately 30 sports encompassing 300+ events. The morning after the announcement of the host venue, the IOC hands over to the leadership team an all-encompassing and comprehensive manual, with all the details and plans that need to be taken into account to make the Games project a success. Almost every aspect is documented, and lessons learned from previous Games are included. Few details are left to chance, including the thorough rehearsals of the opening and the closing ceremonies.

How to put Principle #6 into practice

Quality has to be embedded in the life of the project. Involve the quality experts – internal and/or external – and ensure they commit time to your project. Quality checks, prototyping, testing, rehearsals, etc. all have to be incorporated into the project plan and reported upon. The sooner potential deviations and faults in the end product are found, the less impact they will have on the project's progress, budget and timelines.

Principle #6 highlights the importance of quality when working towards a successful outcome, keeping your eye on what that is at all times. Here are some tools to use, to get you started.

Apply project quality management

According to the Project Management Institute's *Guide to the Project Management Body of Knowledge,* project managers can use the following quality-control tools and techniques to ensure their projects meet quality standards and satisfy stakeholders' and customers' expectations.[5]

- **Cause and effect diagrams:** also known as Ishikawa or fishbone diagrams. These diagrams are used to identify the root cause(s) of potential or existing problems that impact the quality of the project.

- **Flow-charting:** can be used to predict potential flaws in a process flow.
- **Histogram:** a graphical representation of failure frequencies.
- **Run charts:** a series of recorded data over time that is graphically represented. This trend will help in understanding whether there is a problem or not with the outcome of the project.
- **Inspection:** this involves reviewing the product to see if it meets the defined quality standards.
- **Statistical sampling:** measuring a portion (sample) of the entire population instead of measuring the entire population. For example, if you have to inspect 10,000 units a day, then it would take forever to complete the activity. By sampling, it takes much less time.

Embed quality assurance and quality control

As seen with the Olympic Games, achieving success in a project requires a strong focus and no compromise on quality.

Quality in projects is usually split into quality assurance (QA) and quality control (QC). Although QA and QC are closely related concepts, they are distinct.

- Quality control is used to verify the quality of the outputs and end product of the project (defined as 'a part of quality management focused on fulfilling quality requirements').[6]
- Quality assurance is used to verify that the project processes are sufficient (defined as 'a part of quality

management focused on providing confidence that quality requirements will be fulfilled').[7]

Process checklists and project audits are two methods used for project quality assurance. If they are adhered to, the project deliverables will be of good quality.

In simple terms, make sure your project has a process or method to test whatever the project is delivering (whether a product, system, bridge, phone, plane or something else) and that the project plan includes regular quality checks, prototyping and testing time.

10 Principle #7: Well-managed uncertainty is a source of advantage

Anticipate, monitor, mitigate

Principle #7 encourages you to ensure an approach to risk and uncertainty that sustains a tension between pace and assurance.

The online Business Dictionary defines risk as: 'A probability or threat of damage, injury, liability, loss, or any other negative occurrence that is caused by external or internal vulnerabilities, and that may be avoided through pre-emptive action.'

Uncertainty is an inevitable aspect of most projects, but even the most proficient managers have difficulty handling it. Project managers can't predict the future, but applying risk management models to accurately gauge the degree of uncertainty inherent in their projects can help them quickly adapt to it. Thus risk management is one of the most important techniques in project management; it is an essential duty of the project manager, and requires flexibility and sensitivity.

If a project fails unexpectedly, it is because the risks that caused the failure were either not identified or not mitigated in time by the project team.

If a project is being carried out for the first time, superior attention to risks is needed. If a similar type of project is executed again, many of the risks linked to lack of experience diminish, especially if lessons learned are captured.

However, projects are all about risk: doing something you have never done before carries a risk of failure. In that context, the Goldilocks principle of risk management applies: too little risk management and your project may fail; too much risk management and you'll be unable to make any forward progress. Risk management that is just right implies a project team that can flex and adapt their approach in response to the levels of risk at different stages of the project.

Lessons from Tomorrowland

Let's see how risk management is essential at Tomorrowland, one of the largest gatherings in Europe. Tomorrowland is an electronic dance music festival held in Boom, Belgium. It was first held in 2005 and has since become one of the world's largest and most notable music festivals. It now stretches over two weekends and usually sells out in minutes. It is estimated that the 2019 festival will have 500,000 visitors, its highest participation ever.

Having held the event fourteen times diminishes many of the inherent risks; yet the sheer magnitude of such a massive project also generates multiple other threats. Here is a non-exhaustive list of some of the main risks and mitigating actions from the Tomorrowland project.

- **Bad weather, rain, storms, heatwave**
  Keep a close eye on the weather forecast if any strong thunderstorms are expected. Have ponchos ready and provide cover for places when a lot of rain is forecasted.

- **DJ availability**
  Have an extra list with backup DJs who are willing and able to come quickly to Belgium.

- **Electricity shutdown**
  Backup generators will be installed close to all the main stages.

- **Crisis communication**
  Prepare for everything imaginable with extra stable/strong and inflammable tents and have good communication plans ready for different crisis situations. Also have good collaboration and communication plans with police, ambulance and firefighters during the festival.

- **Violence**
  An advance security screening of all the festival people is conducted by local police and access is denied to anyone who poses any safety threat to the festival. Screening of festival-goers is designed to build barriers that serve as protection from attacks.

- **Crowd management**
  Too many people at the same place can result in dramatic scenarios. Advanced cameras will record so-called heat maps to analyse and control crowd movements. When a place becomes too crowded the security personnel will be triggered to go there and move the masses.

The benefits of risk management in projects are huge. If you deal with uncertain project events in a proactive manner, you minimize the impact of project threats, increasing the chances of your project being successful. Doing nothing is rarely a no-risk option, although it can often be seen as such.

Lessons from the Zeebrugge ferry disaster

One of the challenges that organizations have in assessing risk is that one risk is often contingent on another, which means that if something happens and a risk becomes an issue, this issue will either trigger further issues or increase the likelihood or impact of other risks.

This means that it is important not simply to consider and manage your risks in isolation but to look at the scenarios that a particular risk might generate, if triggered.

The correlation between risks is apparent in many accidents. On 6 March 1987, the passenger ferry *Herald of Free Enterprise* capsized and sank soon after leaving Zeebrugge for Dover, with the loss of 150 passengers and 38 of the crew. The subsequent investigation revealed a catalogue of risks, all of which had contributed to the fatal accident.

- The ship was overloaded.
- The crew on duty were not familiar with the officers.
- The design of the ferry made it hard to avoid disaster once she started taking on water.
- The ferry had a sharp turnaround time and accelerated fiercely out of harbour once loaded.
- The assistant bosun, whose responsibility it was to close the inner and outer bow doors, was asleep at the time of departure.

None of these failings on its own would have led to disaster. But cumulatively they did.[1]

How to put Principle #7 into practice

Risk management is basically an approach in which the project team explore, identify, analyse and mitigate those risks that are most likely to affect the project at hand. If done efficiently it will lead to project success.

In large projects, like the construction of a manufacturing plant, risk management is performed by expert risk managers, whose sole role in the project is to build risk models to predict the likelihood of significant risks occurring. For other projects, it is the role of the project leader to perform the risk management activities for the project.

It is important to involve experts, stakeholders and past project team members in early discussions to identify the key risks of the project. Also, assess the risks for the organization of not doing the project. And don't forget to gauge the additional risk that the organization will bear by investing in the project.

Some projects will have thousands of risks, so you don't want to make the risk management process too bureaucratic. Even if it is important to start broadly with the identification of risks, the focus should be on the most likely and most severe risks.

As shown in Figure 3 (overleaf), the sooner the risks are identified and mitigated, where the probability of occurring and severity of impact is extreme, the less costly it will be for the project. A great example of this phenomenon of late risk identification is the French railway operator SNCF, which in 2014 ordered 2,000 new trains that were too big for many of the stations they needed to visit. The train operator admitted

Figure 3: Cost of risk – the later the impact,
the higher the cost

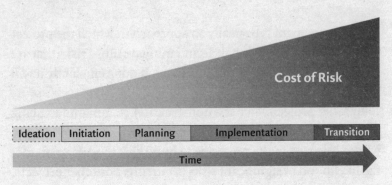

failing to verify measurements before ordering its new stock.
As a result of the mistake, some 1,300 platforms had to be
modified at a cost of €50 million.[2]

As we have seen, Principle #7 encourages an approach to
risk and uncertainty that sustains a tension between pace and
assurance. Here are some tools you can use, to get you started.

Define your organization's risk appetite

One assessment that is often ignored is the additional risk
that a project brings to an already stretched organization. Top
management not only need to look at the risks of one single
project, but the consolidated and integrated portfolio of all the
risks of all the projects run in the organization. Too many risky
projects will generate too much risk in the organization, and
potentially lead to its collapse.

In risk management this is known as the 'risk appetite' – the
amount of risk, on a broad level, an organization is willing to
accept in pursuit of its strategic objectives and before action is

deemed necessary to reduce the risk. It represents a balance between the potential benefits of innovation and the threats that projects inevitably bring. In a literal sense, defining your organization's risk appetite means defining how 'hungry' the organization is for risk.

A carefully managed portfolio of projects will include a number of projects that are closed early because they are no longer needed, some of them in the early stages, and the bulk of projects in execution.

Be proactive with threats that can derail your project

When applying risk management, the risk identification and categorization matrix is the most commonly used tool for assessing the risks that might impact a project. Perform a brainstorming session with the key project stakeholders to identify risks that could impact, or even terminate, the project. Define the importance of each risk by considering the probability or likelihood of the risk occurring and the severity of the impact. This is not a scientific approach, rather a simple mechanism to increase visibility and control of the major risks and take mitigating actions whenever management of the project feel it is appropriate. It does have the advantage that, simply by talking about risk with those involved, you raise the awareness and the profile of risk. And by discussing scenarios and possible options, you can already prepare people to act, if action is required.

Figure 4 is an example of a risk matrix that you can use as a basis to identify and manage the risks in your project. For each risk, identify where it falls on the grid. Those risks that fall into the extreme category are those that you need to focus on. Identify a mitigation plan, but note that mitigating risks

| Figure 4: Project risk assessment matrix

		Impact				
		Trivial	Minor	Moderate	Major	Severe
Probability	Almost certain	Medium	High	High	Extreme	Extreme
	Likely	Medium	Medium	High	High	Extreme
	Possible	Low	Medium	Medium	High	Extreme
	Unlikely	Low	Medium	Medium	Medium	High
	Rare	Low	Low	Medium	Medium	High

has a cost; it will often require extra resources and/or time. As a result, deciding which risks should be mitigated and which should not is something that should be done in discussion with the project team, project sponsor and, eventually, the steering committee.

Always have a Plan B

Include options in your project plan and business case. Options are essentially pre-planned rules – or alternative plans (Plan Bs) – that can be triggered by certain events and threats. Options are rarely mandatory, rather they present the project manager or the project sponsor (depending on the significance of the decision) with choices.

Options can be used to enable remedial action to help recover a potential cost or schedule overrun. Or in the case of a project that is ahead of schedule, or with a budget excess, an option can enable you to add further planned requirements into the project which, hitherto, were not actually scheduled.

Currently the UK's High Speed 2 rail project is facing increasing scrutiny because of growing costs. One of the options for the project is to reduce the speed at which the trains run. Since the main benefit of the HS2 line is not (ironically) speed but rather increased capacity, trading speed against lower cost may be a workable trade-off.

The value of options is the wiggle room they create in your budget and your schedule. If you pre-negotiate additions to or deletions from the project scope, and if you have buy-in from your stakeholders, this enables you to action and initiate those changes without a lengthy process (which might, in itself, delay the project). The rules that you have set for the options to be triggered – 'If X, Y, Z happens (or doesn't happen) then we may trigger option A, B, C' – provide transparency for all involved. Your project team, your sponsor and your stakeholders understand the conditions under which an option may be triggered and they understand what the implications will be if it is.

It is well known that, during the launch of the first iPhone, the new gadget was not fully ready. Yet the demo released on 29 June 2007 at the Apple Convention looked seamless to the audience. The project team at Apple were aware of the risks with the iPhone and mitigated them through detailed risk management. They designed a plan to use several iPhones, one for each key feature (for example, making a call, surfing the internet) throughout the demo. The team rehearsed several times to ensure that there were no last-minute surprises. Despite the challenges, thanks to the detailed risk management, they were able to successfully introduce the iPhone.

Another great example of Plan B is the rescue project of the Chilean miners in the Atacama desert in 2010. The chances of reaching the thirty-three miners alive were slim, and reducing by the hour. The team of experts had identified three possible ways and locations to find them. They could have decided to select one of the three options, try it out and then move to the second one if the first one failed, and so on. As time was of the essence, and in order to reduce the risks, the team decided to implement the three options at the same time. In the end, the third alternative was the one that found them alive. Proactive risk management and options proved to be the drivers for the success of this remarkable project.

11 Principle #8: Stakeholder involvement is required and continual

Identify, communicate, engage

Principle #8 helps you gain an understanding of your stakeholders and their perspectives on the project. Stakeholders are the individuals and groups (entities, organizations, companies) that are impacted by, are involved in or have an interest in the outcome of a project. The larger the project, the more stakeholders there will likely be. The more stakeholders, the more effort is required in terms of communication and change management activities.

Most of us need stability and certainty to feel at ease. Yet the majority of projects involve change, and sometimes disruptive change. Therefore, you should never take it for granted that all (or even the majority) of your stakeholders will be in favour of what you are planning. Even those who support the project in principle may show resistance when they start to experience the degree of change required. As a rule of thumb, the larger the number of people with influence against the project, the more difficult it will be to achieve – although many projects include stakeholders who may be affected by the project or its outcomes but, in practice, wield little power and influence.

Losing the confidence of contractors

The UK Government changed the rules around the tax arrangements for self-employed contractors (IR35 Regulations) in 2017. The new rules were seen by the tax authorities as a way of closing a loophole and bolstering corporate tax revenues. Unfortunately, the new rules in effect prevented self-employed contractors from working for more than two years for the same public sector employer without becoming a permanent member of staff. The majority of contracting staff jealously guarded their independence. The consequence was that many contractors chose to walk away, rather than join the permanent workforce. One source has estimated that many government departments lost up to 40 per cent of their IT contractors over the course of a few months, with a consequential impact on project delivery.

The new regulations will be extended to the private sector in 2020, potentially with a similar impact.

> More than three-quarters (77 per cent) of the 1,400 contractors who took part in a recent poll by IR35 consultancy Qdos said they have little to no confidence that private sector organizations will be ready to manage their new-found responsibilities once the revised IR35 regulations come into effect.[1]

All of which adds up to a spectacularly poorly managed programme, not least because the government departments charged with its implementation failed to engage their stakeholders. Not just the self-employed contractors themselves, but the public sector bodies who had to enact the new rules. The regulations simply adopted a 'blanket' approach to all contractors after two years of self-employment because the time and effort required to differentiate between contractors and identify those who might be exempt (on the basis of the exact work they were doing) was simply too onerous.

By extension, the more powerful or influential the stakeholders, the greater the likely impact of their support or opposition. The sad truth is that there is always someone who will be happy if your project fails.

During the construction of Crossrail, the east–west cross-London railway constructed partly underground, the project team were required to tunnel under the Barbican, a residential and cultural area of London that includes apartments and a number of theatres and concert halls. The project faced considerable opposition from residents' groups and from the powerful City of London Corporation, both of which were concerned about potential noise during the construction and/or the operation of the railway. One of the lessons learned was the significance of which staff Crossrail made available to these stakeholders during the consultations.

> Using senior level specialist and delivery staff instead of communications specialists generated very positive feedback. It was appreciated that we had brought 'the real people' i.e. people with actual responsibility for the project and who were very knowledgeable about what they were delivering.[2]

Your competitors can often be key stakeholders

The stakeholders for Willy Brandt Airport, Berlin Brandenburg, included the state of Brandenburg, the German Federal

Government, the city mayor, the airlines, the passengers, the workers, the citizens of Berlin and the two other Berlin airports. On that basis, it would be fair to assume that some of the people behind Berlin's Tegel and Schönefeld airports didn't mind the massive delays that the Brandenburg project experienced (and continues to experience).

The more stakeholders, the more complex the project and the more effort required in communication and change management matters. The more ambitious the project, in other words – the greater the level of disruption and change required – the greater the potential for opposition to it.

In this case, an upfront identification of the key stakeholders would have helped the project team to understand the stakeholders' needs and interests in the project. In any project, if the resistance is too strong, it is likely that the rationale for the project is not clear enough. To be compelling, it has to address the needs of the groups and people impacted by the project. In certain instances, if there is not enough buy-in from key players, it is better to postpone or not to start the project. Berlin Brandenburg Airport is a good example of a project that should not have started until full engagement from key parties was secured.

Lessons from Stonehenge

Highways England, the body tasked with managing and maintaining the main road arteries of the country, faces a knotty stakeholder problem with its plans to bypass the ancient site of Stonehenge.

The current A303 is the main route from London and the South-East to the South-West of England, including Devon and Cornwall. Unfortunately, the single carriageway road that exists is now hopelessly inadequate for the volume of traffic, particularly during the holiday season. Road users are a powerful lobby that comprises not simply tourists and other private car users but also includes the road haulage industry. Ranged against them are the vocal local inhabitants and then a large body of concerned citizens, as well as the national bodies associated with nature, the environment and English heritage.

Simply tunnelling under the whole area would be prohibitively expensive and might actually exacerbate the damage to the nation's heritage since the area is dotted with burial mounds and other ancient sites.

The project neatly illustrates the problem associated with stakeholder management. The stakeholders in many projects have interests which, while not necessarily diametrically opposed, often involve substantial give and take. You can never please all of the people all of the time and yet, since projects like this are designed for the public good, it is difficult to balance the needs of the stakeholders in such a way as to deliver a cost-effective solution that meets the overall requirements and can mitigate the (unwanted) impact on one or more of the stakeholder groups.[3]

Stakeholders can kill your project

The Uplace Shopping and Leisure Project in Belgium is a case in point. Strongly advocated by the Flemish Government, the plans soon ran into fierce opposition from local and environmental groups.

The plan was to build a complex at Machelen, just outside Brussels in Flemish Brabant province, which would include shops, a hotel, leisure and sporting facilities. But the ambitious plan quickly ran up against opposition: from towns from Vilvoorde to Leuven, who feared a drain of shoppers from their own city centres; from mobility experts, who argued the complex would increase congestion and pollution on the Brussels Ring; from environmental groups, and from rival groups including Neo, which plans a similar complex on the Heysel.

'This final death blow for an outdated project is very good news,' said a spokesperson for the three environmental organizations. 'We have opposed Uplace from the outset. A huge shopping centre at a location accessible only by car is not a solution to the challenges of air pollution, climate, traffic and town planning.'[4]

Those running construction and infrastructure projects need to be very sensitive to the risk of opposition from an alliance of local groups, concerned about the impact on their quality of life, and national or sometimes international groups, concerned about the environment, social justice or other, often very emotive, causes.

People tend to be reluctant to change

Change management is about ensuring that the key stakeholders, the organization and its employees are ready to embrace the changes introduced by a project. Communication is one of the most important aspects of managing change successfully. Based on their stakeholder analysis, the project leader needs to define the types of information that will be delivered, who will receive it, how best to communicate it, and the timing of its release and distribution. According to the Project Management Institute's *Guide to the Project Management Body of Knowledge*, between 75 and 90 per cent of a project manager's time is spent formally or informally communicating during the implementation phase of a project.[5]

According to the PMI's *Pulse of the Profession* report (an annual global survey about trends in project management), highly effective communicators are more likely to deliver projects on time and within budget.[6]

To advance a project, it is important that everybody gets the right messages at the right times. The first step is to find out what kind of information and/or intervention each stakeholder group needs to embrace the changes introduced by the project. It is important to inform them about the reality and the status of the project, rather than painting a rosy picture of the future. Communications to stakeholders may consist of good news, bad news or sometimes 'no news'. Prolonged silence is likely to encourage stakeholders to worry and so, in some cases, such as when awaiting a decision, a holding communication to reassure them that nothing has changed can be extremely valuable.

Nowadays, technology has a major impact on how people are kept in the loop. Methods of change management can take many forms, such as written updates, newsletters, face-to-face meetings, presentations, town hall meetings, mentoring sessions, a project website and so on.

The main challenge is not to bury stakeholders in too much information, but you do want to give them enough so that they're informed, can make appropriate decisions and have a clear and meaningful platform to allow their ideas and concerns to be heard.

Lessons from the launch of the euro

One of the best examples of major change management happened in Europe on 1 January 1999, with the introduction of its new currency, the euro. Originally, the euro was an overarching currency used for exchange between countries within the Union, while each nation continued to use its own currency. Within three years, however, the euro was established as an everyday currency and had replaced the domestic currencies of the member states of the Eurozone. During the years prior to the introduction, as well as during the transition, almost all European citizens knew about the project and were fully prepared for the change. Their backgrounds, nationalities, ages and other characteristics didn't matter – they knew the key dates and the benefits the euro would bring to them, and they even knew the conversion rate between their existing currency and the euro.

The project had two key success factors. First, European leaders were anxious to use communication to ensure the population of Europe was ready for the change. Second, they ensured the project was done in an extremely simple way, so that every single citizen, irrespective of their education and culture, would understand the purpose, benefits, implications and timing of the euro conversion project.

How to put Principle #8 into practice

The shift from hard project management skills to soft and the increase in the complexity of projects have made stakeholder management one of the areas that requires the most attention.

Understanding the needs of the key stakeholders, identifying win-wins and aligning stakeholders to actively support the project are key for project success, but they can be daunting tasks. The project manager needs to engage the executive sponsor, who plays a major role in stakeholder management.

In addition, all projects require a sound change management plan. But not all projects will have the same types of activities or the same methods for distributing and communicating the information. The project plan should document:

- the types of information and change needs the stakeholders have
- when the information should be distributed or stakeholder needs addressed, and
- how the interventions will be delivered.

You need to prioritize the change and communication activities and convey the right amount of information. Too much communication can be overwhelming, leading to important information getting lost. On the other hand, too little communication may not provide a clear enough picture to allow team members to complete the work that needs to be done. Project managers who understand how to send the right amount of information to the right people at the right time will be able to keep things moving smoothly, resulting in a successful project.

Principle #8 highlights the importance of starting with an understanding of your stakeholders and their understanding of the project, and sustaining this throughout the process. Here are some tools you can use, to get you started.

Use the stakeholder analysis matrix

This matrix is the most frequently used for weighing and balancing the interests of those who are impacted by or involved in the changes a project will bring about. Whenever possible, stakeholder analysis needs to identify their concerns and their requirements, if the project is to meet its objectives. Whereas risk appraisal should be carried out with a larger group, stakeholder analysis should be performed in small groups. Some of the discussions can be sensitive, and there is a danger that adopting definitions of stakeholder groups that are too broad and unsophisticated will alienate anyone who feels the detail of their concerns is being ignored.

| Figure 5: Project stakeholder analysis matrix

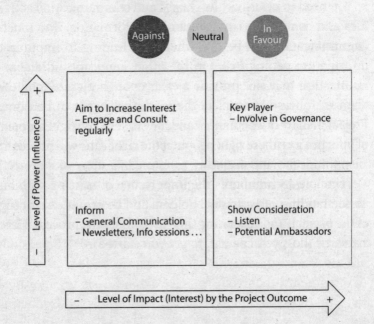

The initial assessment is usually performed during the preparation phase by the project leader with the project sponsor. Once the major stakeholders have been identified, each group or individual is categorized according to three dimensions. The first is the level of interest (positive or negative) in the project or its outcome. The second is the level of influence (positive or negative) that the stakeholder could have on the project. This dimension is often also linked to the power of the individual or group in the organization. The third is using the colour coding RAG (red, amber and green) to indicate the stakeholder's current position towards the project.

The analysis should be repeated on a regular basis to track the changes in stakeholders' attitudes over time. Figure 5 (opposite) is an example of a stakeholder matrix that you can use as a basis to identify and address the stakeholders impacted by and involved in your project.

Draw up a change management plan

This will enable you to engage the organization and individuals.

There are two types of change management plans. One addresses the impact of change to an organization, easing the transition. The other tracks changes to a single project, creating a clear record of product tweaks or alterations to the project scope. Both of these plans aim to communicate what needs to be done clearly and accurately.

If you understand the difference between those responsible for delivering a change process (usually the project team) and those ultimately accountable for it (the decision makers), and between those who need to be consulted before any decisions are made and those who simply wish to be kept abreast of developments, then you will have a good basis for allocating the work and planning your communications for facilitating the change. It will allow you to ensure that you do not overlook anyone and that you structure, tailor and time communication in a way that is appropriate and most useful for each of the groups. Remember, ill-timed or poorly framed communication can be just as damaging as no communication at all.

When introducing the euro, the European Commission (EC) developed a detailed change management plan, in every language of the European Union, which included information packs, visuals, commercials, toolkits and so on. Here are some examples that you can use as a basis for your transformation projects.

- *Preparing the Introduction of the Euro: A Short Handbook*
- *Communication Toolkit*[7]

In addition, the EC created a comprehensive website that included all relevant information. Most of the communication material has been used every time new member states have joined the euro.

Understand the Change Curve

The Change Curve is widely used in business and change management to support individuals embracing the new reality. It is attributed to psychiatrist Elisabeth Kübler-Ross, resulting from her work on personal transition in grief and bereavement. The model describes the five stages most people go through as they adjust to change.

When a significant change is first introduced in an organization, people's initial reaction may be shock or denial, as they react to the challenge to the status quo (Stage 1).

Once the reality of the change starts to hit, people tend to react negatively and move to Stage 2. They may fear the impact, feel angry, and actively resist or protest against the changes. As a result, the organization experiences disruption which, if not carefully managed, can quickly spiral into chaos. In Stage 3 people realize that the change is inevitable and the anger will lead to depression. People may reach a point of feeling de-motivated and uncertain about their future. For as long as most employees resist the change, the project will be unsuccessful. This is a stressful and unpleasant stage.

In Stage 4 employees start to let go, and accept the changes. They begin testing and exploring what the new reality means, and how they must adapt.

By Stage 5, people not only accept the changes but also start to embrace them: they rebuild their ways of working. Only when employees get to this stage can the organization really start to reap the benefits of change.

12 Principle #9: A high-performing team and culture are indicators of the health and resilience of a project

Team, project, organization

Principle #9 encourages you to invest time to develop techniques for measuring and sustaining your team's motivation, capability and performance.

The shifting focus of success

Today, project managers need to be project leaders too, especially for the more complex and cross-functional projects. These require pulling together resources from across the organization and changing the old status quo. In fact, we can argue that the best project managers are not only leaders but also entrepreneurs – they are the CEOs of their projects.

Marshall Goldsmith, the world's number-one executive coach, told me, 'Executives tend to see project managers as technical experts: very tactical people, focused on the detailed challenges of the project. Modern leadership is moving into facilitation. The best CEOs I have coached are great facilitators. Therefore, the project managers of the future will have to become project leaders, strong in facilitation, rather than technical experts.'[1]

Over the past decades, we have seen the focus shifting from

the original areas of project management, also known as hard skills (scope, planning, scheduling and estimation), to soft skills (leadership, stakeholder management and communication). A good project manager can navigate the organization, motivate the team, sell the project's benefits to the key stakeholders, and deliver on scope, on time and within budget. Other skills required by successful project managers are:

- understanding the strategic and business aspects of the project
- influencing and persuading stakeholders at all levels
- leading in a matrix organization
- creating a high-performing team from a group of individuals
- providing feedback and motivating the project team, and
- monitoring the progress of the project work.

Understanding the individual and the team

During the development of a huge and technologically advanced new commuter train station at London Bridge, in the heart of the UK's capital, Costain, one of the main contractors, understood that everyone involved on the project needed to be listened to as an individual in order to see themselves as part of a team.

The concrete piling contractors were not initially familiar with the greater safety demands of such a complex site. Initial attempts to improve safety by 'calling out' poor safety practice or using disciplinary procedures proved counter-productive, encouraging the staff involved to become defensive and resentful.

Instead, the project team started to take time to understand how and why the contractors were working in the ways they were, and then took time to demonstrate why and how the demands of the London Bridge site were different.

Projects are often seen as a development opportunity for high-potential managers. They take the lead of a large strategic project for two years to get exposure with top management. At the same time, they build complementary skills not required in a line function. The problem is that they don't see projects as a long-term career, and thus they are not interested in learning about project management in more depth. So they struggle, as they are not aware of the tools and techniques that will make the project a success.

The integrated project team

Construction projects are traditionally organized around a client who contracts the building work to a main contractor who, in turn, subcontracts elements of the project to a long supply chain of smaller companies.

These projects struggle to innovate and often find themselves mired in painful litigation between different contractors and the client over unfulfilled responsibilities.

The response of the industry in the face of the growing size and complexity of projects has been to endeavour to re-engineer their contracting process and to create integrated project teams.

Some owners are successfully applying a fresh alternative approach to the way they are contracting and incentivizing their project teams to collaborate. They are using a form of contract that involves more than two parties to the agreement: a 'multi-party contract' that allows multiple parties to all agree to a common set of terms and expectations. At a minimum, the owner, its architect and its contractor all sign the single agreement, and in some cases, other members of the project team that are deemed to be critical to the project success are also brought into the multi-party agreement. Besides the parties all signing a single agreement, what is also unique is how risks are shared and how compensation is tied not to an individual party's performance, but rather the team's performance on the overall project. Integration of project teams is proving to yield better results.[2]

Another aspect to consider is project staffing. Projects need people to carry them out. Ensuring that the organization has available resources, with the right skills, expertise and experience to implement the project, is an essential responsibility of senior management. Yet it is surprising to see how many organizations launch projects without doing a capacity check prior to confirming the initiative.

The best and most experienced staff (for example, developers) may be booked on other tasks and projects. If their contribution is not suitably planned, the project is going to suffer. Lack of availability of required resources leads to delays and frequently to project failure.

Besides availability, a key aspect of project success is team commitment. As mentioned earlier, people tend to have other responsibilities besides their contribution to the project. Commitment to the project is never a given, especially because employees are often asked to join in such a way that it is difficult for them to refuse (we've all received an email that asks us to 'kindly' agree to something but where in reality we don't have much choice). They are ready to contribute, often for free and/or giving up some of their private time, only because they want to be part of an amazing experience.

Project managers may be asked to complete extensive and often time-consuming reports to inform senior management about the progress of a project. Yet a quick and easy way to assess the health of a project is by asking the project manager two questions.

1 How much time do you dedicate to this project?
2 How committed are you to the project?

Ideally, the answer to both should be 100 per cent, which increases the chances of success. However, often project managers are not fully dedicated to one single project. Depending on the project, 50 per cent is still acceptable, but anything below that will increase the risk of failure due to potentially feeble oversight and weak management.

The importance of interaction

Kelvin McGrath, founder of an Australian organization called Meeting Quality, understood intuitively that the health of a project could be tracked by understanding the quality of the social interactions – most obviously the project meetings – and how it fluctuates at different times during the project.

Using classic social network analysis tools to map the number of interactions within an organization (and who was interacting with whom) allowed him to build a picture of the culture of the organizations with which he was working.

Later he realized that actually the quality of these interactions was much more important than the quantity alone. He created an algorithm called the Meeting Promoter Score (MPS), which allowed the quality of interactions to be measured between individuals and more importantly groups of individuals. Individual MPS scores could then be aggregated for the organization and beyond.[3]

Lessons from Apple's approach to team selection

'We're starting a new project,' he told them. 'It's so secret, I can't even tell you what the new project is. I cannot tell you who you will work for. What I can tell you is that if you choose to accept this role, you're going to work harder than you ever have in your entire life. You're going to have to give up nights and weekends probably for a couple of years as we make this product.'[4]

So Scott Forstall, head of the iPhone software division, might have approached his potential project team members. The project team comprised one of the most talented groups of individuals in recent history. The best engineers, the best programmers and the best designers were selected to join the team. And not part time – one day, or half a day a week – which is most companies' standard approach with their strategic projects. The chosen people were fully discharged from all their duties and were assigned full time to the project, effective immediately. Project Purple became their life.

Forstall later explained that Steve Jobs had told him he could have anyone in the company on his team. And the high quality of the team didn't stop with the technicians. Jobs decided to include the best leadership team too, starting with Jonny Ive, the designer of the iPod and MacBook, who was put in charge of the look of the handset.[5]

How to put Principle #9 into practice

At the beginning of a project, senior management need to assess and confirm the capacity to work on the project. They need to ensure the resources and the skills required to develop the solution are there. It is necessary to anticipate potential bottlenecks by freeing up resources or engaging external capacity and expertise.

Establish a standard process to appoint the best-prepared project manager to lead the project. They should have technical knowledge of project management, the required leadership competencies and business understanding. The organization should recognize project management as a task for professional project managers; develop a project management competency framework and an official career path to help project managers grow in the role.

Principle #9 highlights the importance of team culture as an indicator of the health and resilience of a project. Here are some tools you can use, to get you started.

Select an engaged and dedicated team
This should include the project leader and sponsor. Ask the project leader two questions to help assess whether the project is in good hands.

- **How much of your time do you dedicate to this project?**
  Strategic projects require 100 per cent dedication. Anything below that can lead to distraction and to a reduction in the pressure on the project. Often project managers are asked to lead several projects simultaneously. In my experience, it is hard to lead more than three important projects at the same time, and it is also hard, not to say impossible, to manage an important project while having a full-time position in the day-to-day activities of the organization.

- **How committed are you to the success of the project?**
  Knowing that the project will face challenges, if the project manager and resources are not committed, the project will most likely be a total failure. A great example of the positive thinking required is Alan Mulally, the project manager in charge of building the Boeing 777, a massive undertaking, in the worst circumstances, after the terrorist attacks of 11 September 2001, and with Boeing struggling to survive. Yet his strong commitment and full-time dedication drove a project of 10,000 team members to create one of the most advanced aircraft in the world.

Lack of conviction in a project leader can quickly spread to the rest of the team. When the conviction and morale drop significantly, the sponsor should intervene and find ways to restore confidence, either by taking corrective actions or, eventually, by replacing the project manager.

Proactively foster a high-performing team

High-performing teams work together to convey exceptional project outcomes, over and over again. High-performing teams don't happen just by coincidence or chance. Research around team dynamics has identified several common characteristics. The performance of the group is based on:

- instituting shared trust and respect
- a comprehension of the individuals, their different backgrounds and practices, and
- an alignment on a common purpose.

One of the main reasons why project teams are not highly productive, therefore impacting the performance of the project, is because the project leader doesn't build this foundation in the early stages of the project.

The best project leaders set aside time at the beginning of the project for the team to:

- become acquainted with one another
- participate in the setting of the goals of the project
- hold each other accountable for meeting these goals
- build trust across the team, and
- establish a set of ground rules that will define the required behaviours for the team.

An important aspect to consider when forming the team is that the most engaged members of a project are, in most cases, those who voluntarily join the project.

The four stages that a team need to go through to reach the high-performing stage are:

- stage 1 – forming
- stage 2 – storming
- stage 3 – norming
- stage 4 – performing.

Here is a checklist you can apply for high-performing teams.

- **Introduction**
  The team have the time to meet and get to know each other.

- **Goal setting**
  All team members participate in establishing the project and team goals.

- **Ground rules**
  The team have defined expectations about team behaviour and values, which have been written down and shared.

- **Team identity**
  The team can describe their primary purpose and expected goals. The team win and lose, not individuals.

- **Contribution**
  The members have responsibilities in their area of expertise, and are aware of how they can actively contribute to achieving the goals of the project.

- **Problem solving and risk taking**
  The team have a problem-solving culture and are encouraged to take risks. Individuals are not blamed or punished.

- **Joint decision making**
  The team are capable of making decisions that are backed by all the members in a timely manner.

- **Conflict handling**
  Team members feel free to voice conflicting points of view, including when they disagree with the project leader. Conflicts are resolved in a timely and direct fashion, with no damage to relationships and with the best possible outcome.

- **Feedback**
  Both the team and individuals receive feedback regularly; there is a continuous improvement mindset.

- **Leadership**
  The project leader and sponsor are the first ones applying the high-performing rules.

13 Principle #10: Project-driven organizations build capability to deliver change

Selection, prioritization, implementation, agility

The final principle relates to the organization itself and focuses on designing systems and processes for managing the portfolio, developing the team and aligning the organization.

Most Western companies have a hierarchical and functional structure, which is ideal for running their daily business activities in a more or less stable and predictive world. Budgets, resources, key performance indicators and decision-making power are 'owned' by the heads of business units, departments and functions.

However, the largest and most critical projects – the strategic ones – are cross-functional and cross-hierarchical by nature: they cut across the organization. This means that a strategic project, such as expanding the business into another country or digital transformation, requires resources and input from a number of different departments and functions. Facilities experts find the location, lawyers handle the legal documents, HR experts recruit the people, salespeople develop a commercial plan, and so forth. Without the timely contributions of all these departments, the project will not succeed.

A key element of a project-driven organization

Within the traditional hierarchical organizational structure, quick project execution is not possible. The most successful organizations today have adjusted their structure to facilitate and support the execution of projects. They have become project driven: resources, budgets and decision-making power have partially shifted to the project activities, often driven by the implementation of a corporate Project Management Office (PMO).

The initial purpose of a PMO was to support the project leader and the project team in the administrative tasks of the projects, such as tracking timesheets, maintaining issue logs and chasing information in order to provide progress reports. The role then evolved towards an office in charge of the development and implementation of policies and standards on project management. This strong focus on 'administrative tasks' created a negative perception of the value of these PMOs, which commonly led to them being dismantled (on average, they lasted only up to three years).

The more recent iteration of the PMO has a stronger focus on value creation. They are now linked to the executive team. Their role has evolved into enterprise or portfolio PMOs and now includes promoting and establishing best practice, building competencies, supporting the top levels of management in prioritizing projects, and executing the most strategic projects. The most advanced PMOs have a series of project managers, often the best in the company, who are in charge of leading the most complex and transversal (company-wide) initiatives. In many cases, the office reports to the CEO, so it is sometimes called a CEO Office.

A great example of the power of the PMO comes from a leading Swiss biotech company. The CEO's goal was to grow revenues by €1 billion by 2022. He established a transformation PMO and selected one of the brightest people in the management team to lead it. She reported to the CEO. The executive team, with the support of the PMO head, selected thirteen strategic initiatives. They appointed the most talented people, who received extensive executive training. Nine out of the thirteen initiatives are on track and starting to deliver some benefits, and the company is on course to deliver the CEO's target.

Lessons from LEGO bricks

For pretty much anyone from the baby boomer generation onwards, the Danish toy company LEGO is synonymous with growing up. But in the early 2000s, the company was in trouble and nearly ran out of road. They had expanded their range in all sorts of fairly random directions; they were carrying the cost of manufacturing and storing huge amounts of different parts for different construction kits; and they had little or no sense of how much certain sets cost to manufacture, nor of how profitable they were.

> Jorgen Vig was put in charge, he made the hard call and made redundancies, they slashed the number of parts down to 6000 (a figure that has grown, but [is] still well below the 2003 total) – the company reorganized and analyzed all costs, design was finally linked to manufacturing cost and re-focused on the core business of making construction sets. The unprofitable LEGO Computer games business was shut down.[1]

The company then re-engineered its creative design approach. Many of the new designers it had recruited to replace the baby boomer generation, who were responsible for the company's success in the twentieth century but had since retired, were great designers but knew little about LEGO building. To counter this problem, they took the bold move to put creative control of the business into the hands of hard-core fans.

The LEGO story illustrates many of the features of major projects in the twenty-first century.

- The tendency for businesses to launch far too many projects, products and ideas, instead of focusing on the most valuable.
- The need for a transformed business organization as much as for new products and services.
- The role of business change in product and service development.

How to put Principle #10 into practice

Consistently excelling in project execution requires strong project management capabilities. Resources dedicated to leading projects have to be trained and certified, with the role considered as a profession. A career path and a training development programme are also musts.

The Swiss biotech company I referred to earlier engaged one of the leading executive education schools to design a tailor-made development programme for its most talented soon-to-be project leaders. The programme's backbone was project management, but it also included leadership, finance, team development and communication sessions. Additionally, it incorporated several sessions on the biotech's own business (for example, new products in the pipeline) and about the technological future. It required strong commitment from the participants, as it was run over three sets of four-day sessions, held over the course of a year. It was a huge investment for the company but a great development opportunity. It clearly showed the CEO's firm commitment to investing in talent to deliver his ambition through project excellence.

Principle #10 highlights the importance of building capability across the organization to deliver change. Here are some tools you can use, to help you get started.

Establish a company-wide prioritization process

Projects that are top priority for an organization or country always have a better chance of being delivered successfully. For example, projects relating to the introduction of the Global Data Protection Regulation (GDPR) by the European Commission in 2018, which had a fixed deadline and mandatory adherence, were high priority in most organizations.[2] The regulation aims to give EU citizens control of their personal data. Companies knew they needed to comply to avoid punishment, so managers readily committed resources to the project.

Prioritizing increases the success rates of strategic projects. It increases the alignment and focus of senior management teams around strategic goals, clears all doubts for the operational teams when faced with decisions and, most importantly, builds an execution mindset and culture.

Despite the importance of having a prioritized list of projects, the reality is that most organizations and governments struggle to prioritize. Many don't even have a list of all the projects they are carrying out. Prioritization means saying 'no' to many potential ideas, or cancelling projects previously started. Most successful companies clearly know what their top projects are, and are extremely disciplined in those projects' execution.

One of the most challenging aspects of prioritization is that often all of the potential projects and ideas do make sense, yet there are constraints regarding resources and budgets. Even more importantly, the more projects there are, the harder it is to deliver them successfully.

Most companies only prioritize when they enter a crisis and are on the brink of collapse. Famous examples are Apple, LEGO, the Ford Motor Company, Boeing, Philips and Unilever. Only when the executive teams put pressure on these companies were they able to scrap hundreds of projects and products, and focus on the ones that were essential – often the ones that had made the company successful.

To explain the strategic relevance of prioritization and assist executives in the process, I developed a model called the Hierarchy of Purpose, which uses the company purpose as the main driver to select projects.[3]

Appoint a Chief Project Officer and establish a Project Investment Committee

Perhaps the best example of how project management is impacting the way organizations are structured is the appearance of a new role, that of Chief Project Officer.

The Chief Project Officer is in charge of establishing and running a governing body – the Project Investment Committee or Project Review Board – that decides which ideas and initiatives the organization should invest in, but also decides which projects should be stopped or delayed, and oversees the successful execution and thus the creation of value for the company. The positioning of the committee within the organization and the members who participate in the committee will determine, to a great extent, the impact and success of the entire project portfolio management framework. It is recommended that the chair of the committee should be the company's CEO. The rest of the members should be the executive team. The Chief Project Officer is a board-level executive who is the embodiment of the project organization.[4]

The Project Investment Committee should report to the board's risk committee and provide regular updates to the board via the CEO. It is important to note that very few companies manage to implement a portfolio management framework across all their departments; they are usually implemented within IT, R&D, supply chain or technical departments. In order to work as intended, the Chief Project Officer should oversee all the strategic projects, breaking silos and ensuring that people work more closely together as one company. The Chief Project Officer should have strong analytical skills, sound project management experience and excellent business knowledge. Communication and persuasion skills are also essential, as most of their time will be dedicated to talking to key stakeholders from different levels in the organization.

Establish a Central Project Management Office

The Chief Project Officer will lead the CEO Office, also called Central Project Management Office, or Strategy Execution Office, which will be composed of the best project leaders in the organization. The office's mission is to provide oversight to the organization's portfolio of strategies and the projects that support them, as well as other responsibilities.

- Helping to ensure that every strategy is sense-checked to make sure that it is, indeed, something that can be effectively delivered through a project or a programme.
- Tracking the success of these strategic projects once they are delivered and feeding back data so that the portfolio can be balanced and the projects within it accelerated, slowed or changed.

14 From project manager to project leader

What skills are required to become a successful project leader in today's fast-changing world?

In a world that will have ever-increasing numbers of projects, the demand for strong project implementation competencies is increasing by the hour. Just search on LinkedIn and it will be clear that more and more job descriptions require sound project management skills and experience. In two of my previous companies, one of the major skill gaps identified was the lack of people capable of leading projects across the organization, also known as managing in the matrix. Although we learn several of those skills throughout our lives by intuition and practice – and many could claim to be project leaders already – the reality is that the core skills have to be learned and taught.

The project leader of the future will be a *chef d'orchestre*, a football coach, a true team player; someone who is able to gather a diverse group of people, each with their own expertise, and create a high-performing team out of the different individuals. Each participant has to have a clear role, feel that they are contributing to the purpose of the project and be appreciated by the others. I strongly believe that anyone can develop into a successful project leader. However, it requires focus, commitment, determination, personal awareness, eagerness to learn and perseverance during times of failure. I group the main qualities needed to excel in the project-driven world into five categories.

1. Essential project management skills

A good project leader should be able to use the available tools and techniques to determine the rationale and business case of a project. They should be able to work with key contributors and partners in defining the scope (whether for a detailed design, technical solution, product or service). The ability to break down the scope into manageable workloads – to identify interdependencies, to prioritize the work and translate the work into a comprehensive project plan – is one of the most important skills in these categories. Everyone can make a plan, but very few can make a well-defined and precise plan. It requires a good understanding of the details (analytical skills), as well as the overall picture (strategic skills).

Risk identification and risk management techniques are also essential. Once the project is under way, the project leader needs to establish reporting mechanisms to monitor the execution of the plan and ensure that sufficient quality checks and tests are being carried out. When delays are foreseen, or changes to the plan, a good project leader should be able to analyse the consequences and provide viable alternatives to the sponsor and steering committee.

How to acquire these competencies

My recommendation is to follow a training programme on project management and implementation. There are also year-long masters courses available. Just be aware that their content is focused on the added value, rather than pure and traditional technical project management. Ultimately, the goal is to obtain a recognized certification that accredits your knowledge. The most common worldwide accreditation is Project Management Professional (PMP) certification, from the Project Management Institute. There are others, such as PRINCE2 practitioner certification, which is well recognized in the UK and Commonwealth countries. A final option comes from the International Project Management Association, which is not as well known, but which offers a competency framework that is a good complement.

2. Technical expertise

These competencies give the project leader credibility among the team and the project stakeholders. They help the leader to have a minimum understanding of the important technical aspects of the project, and provide the ability to communicate in the language of the technicians. The technical skills of the project leader do not need to be too advanced, as this can lead to the tendency to end up deciding on and doing most of the work. A certain level of understanding, enough to challenge the teams, is enough. For example, if the project is to implement a new performance monitoring application, the project leader should take the time to get their head around some of the technical aspects of the software.

How to acquire these competencies

Be curious and open-minded. The bare minimum when starting a project in an unknown domain is to dedicate some time to reading articles, watching videos and looking at analysts' reports. There may be online training via some of the MOOC (Massive Open Online Course) sites now available from many universities and professional business associations. Meet experts if you have access to them. Learn some of the key words and some of the major challenges faced in the industry. Make a summary of what you find out.

Never be afraid to admit that you are new to the industry or the topic. Highlight that you are eager to learn and appreciate the patience of the people who are giving you information. Don't forget to explain your added value and what you will bring to the project.

3. Strategy and business acumen

Develop a good understanding of the environment in which the project will be implemented. For example, if the project is about increasing access to education, a good project leader will need to have a good appreciation of the different educational systems – which are the most successful, why, and what are the alternatives that best fit the specific needs that the project wants to address. Similarly, in terms of business projects, the project leader should have a minimum understanding of the business, its purpose, its strategy and goals, its main products or services, its key competitors and its main challenges. Additional knowledge of these functions is an asset.

Financial understanding is also a must. Being able to connect the project outcomes and purpose to concrete business challenges and priorities is essential for project buy-in and success. Most of the stakeholders, including senior management, will be more supportive towards the project and the project leader whenever that connection is made. The most important capability in this category is to ensure that, from the early stages, the project has a strong focus on the benefits and the impact. Value creation is one of the most critical and sought-after skills in the project-driven world.

How to acquire these competencies

When dealing with projects in the business world, the best way to acquire these skills is through a Master of Business Administration (MBA) degree. MBA programmes are not cheap and require a significant time commitment, yet they cover most relevant aspects of management in general, and provide a strong general understanding of the key facets of a business.

Alternatively, there are masters programmes and even on-line courses (many free) on specific topics (innovation, finance, strategy, etc.), which are a good complement for a project manager.

4. Leadership skills

The increased speed of change, the higher complexity, the overlapping priorities, the conflicting objectives, the culture of searching for a consensus, the multiple generations now working at the same time – all these important elements make the implementation of projects much harder than in the past. While pure managerial skills were largely sufficient for previous generations, today, management skills are not enough; project managers have to evolve towards project leadership. They have to be able to provide direction, which requires the ability to:

- communicate progress and changes
- evaluate, develop and motivate staff
- deal effectively with people, without having authority, by motivating them (working in a matrix)

- confront and challenge
- engage the project sponsor and senior leadership
- understand different cultures and how to leverage from them
- manage and persuade multiple stakeholders, sometimes ones who are against the project
- build bridges across the organization (which will often be silo-driven and scarce in resources)
- create a high-performing team, and
- dedicate enough time to develop and coach team members.

In addition, a modern project leader has to be able to make effective decisions, be proactive, have discipline and be results-driven. Last but not least, a project leader has to be resilient, which is the ability to bounce back from any difficulties and changes that life throws their way – probably one of the most important leadership skills in projects.

As Lao Tzu, one of the most famous Chinese philosophers, said in his book *Tao Te Ching* (*The Way of Life*), 'A leader is best when people barely know he exists, when his work is done, his aim fulfilled, they will say: we did it ourselves.'[1]

How to acquire these competencies

Leadership skills are the most difficult to teach and to develop. Some of them, such as communication, are easier to learn than others but most of them require awareness, time, practice and perseverance. There are various models that you can use to get an understanding of the topic.[2]

The most important step to start growing in this area is to be aware of your personal characteristics and your strengths and weaknesses. Accept that you are not great at everything. Select one or two areas you want to develop over the next year. You can work on them alone (self-development), follow a specialized course and/or engage a personal coach.

Open access learning and development
Praxis is a free framework for the management of projects, programmes and portfolios. It includes a body of knowledge, a methodology, a competency framework and a capability maturity model. The framework is supported by a knowledge base of resources and an encyclopaedia.

The framework has recently added a diagnostic that allows you to identify your preferred working style so that you can understand how you are most comfortable working within a team and in collaboration with others.[3] The results of the diagnostic have been mapped to the original Praxis framework and show you the impact of your personal style on elements within the project process (for example, assurance, benefits, risk and stakeholder management).

5. Ethics and values

Project leaders are expected to have strong ethics and personal values. Leadership involves a relationship between people. Therefore, the ability to influence others ethically is a major indicator of effective leaders.

Leaders are often in the spotlight and become role models for the team members and the organization. In the project-driven world, there is less room for hiding and mismanagement, as projects and their implementation tend to be very visible and to require quick thinking.

Ethics, the motivation to act as a role model, and developing a plan of action are key aspects that positively affect leadership and a project's outcome. When ethics and values are made a priority and are respected, it will have a positive effect on leadership.

How to acquire these competencies

Ethics cannot be acquired – they are part of who we are. However, you can develop a code of ethics that will act as a moral guide for you and for your project. This will also help to guide the project team on ethical matters. To develop a code of ethics for you or the project, look at examples of codes of ethics from other people and other companies. Then identify your own values by asking the following questions.

- What are my true beliefs?
- How would I like others to be treated?
- How would I like to treat others?

Share the outcome with your team and discuss whether they feel comfortable with these values. Once the project's code of ethics has been approved, it should be applied and followed by every member of the project, starting with you. Nowhere is the aphorism of 'leading by example' more important than in the area of ethics.

Making sense of the project manager's code of ethics

In 2015, the International Project Management Association published their first ever 'Code of Ethics and Professional Conduct'. The code offered a series of statements relating to stakeholders and the wider project environment, including a fundamental principle.

We acknowledge that our community and the relations between professionals and their clients depend upon trust, mutual respect and the appreciation of our diversity.

We welcome the fact that we, as members of this community and as professionals, work in environments that are charged with various sensitive political, cultural and moral challenges, and we believe we are best equipped to embrace those challenges by being open to and respectful of our differences.

When working with clients, project owners and other stakeholders we act with integrity, accountability and transparency. We realize that our work in project, programme or project portfolio management may present us with a variety of ethical challenges and we believe that it is through these values that we will best be able to meet them.[4]

15 Start thriving with your projects

Putting into practice the 10 Principles to succeed in today's project-driven world

Fundamental transformations, such as changing the company's values and culture, always require a big investment of time, money and effort, and their benefits are very difficult to quantify. Often, the benefits are of the so-called soft – or intangible – variety, such as an improvement in motivation, or the creation of an entrepreneurial mindset. The hard benefits, like cost savings or revenue increases, are frequently not concrete. In addition, gains are generally achieved in the medium to long term, usually after three to five years of hard work.

Because CEOs and top management receive substantial pressure from their key stakeholders – shareholders and stock markets in for-profit organizations; citizens for government institutions – to show quick and steady, positive returns on their investments, they are reluctant to embark on long-term and deep transformation initiatives. Instead, they prefer to invest in projects which pay off much more quickly and have a tangible impact.

Usually, the parallel launch of a transformation project and a strategic project is what top management regards as the most attractive scenario. This is a controllable situation, if management focuses just on these two initiatives. However, as explained before, they often end up launching too many strategic and operational projects simultaneously or in a short time period, which is a recipe for failure.

This final chapter describes in practical terms the steps necessary to implement the 10 Principles of Project Success. To overcome the two major drawbacks to the process of transforming your organization's capability to deliver projects – intangible benefits and a delay in achieving them – I have developed a fast-track approach using the 10 Principles that provides top management with quantifiable results in less than twelve months. To achieve the full benefits of any transformation, the outcomes from the project have to be consolidated and the changes have to be fully embedded in the company.

Let's summarize how the 10 Principles can be used to transform your organization.

#1: Everything starts with ideation

Your organization has been running projects for years, so don't throw away all that wealth of experience that exists in-house. Identify and capture the current best practices around the project principles. It is possible that they exist only in some areas of the organization. That doesn't matter. In terms of change, it is easier to adjust and spread an organization's own practices than to introduce completely new concepts from outside.

Don't go for a full-blown, big bang approach when introducing this new way of working. Piloting and continuous iteration are parts of the process. It is important to start small; plan two or three pilots that will use the 10 Principles. Let the project leader and team experiment and fine-tune the approach to make it specific to your organization.

#2: A clear purpose informs and inspires

Ask yourself how the company will benefit from the implementation. Each level of the organization will benefit in a different way. The exact nature and level of benefits will depend on two factors.

1 Your current capability compared to your planned future capability.
2 The extent to which your organization is shifting from being operationally to project focused.

It is important that your organization achieves a transformation that gives it the right level of project capability and resources. Too few resources and you'll struggle to keep up and compete with your peers; too many and you'll become wasteful or may be tempted to undertake too many projects, simply because you have the people.

In addition, the following benefits can be expected by implementing the 10 Principles of Project Success.[1]

- 15 per cent reduction in projects that fail to deliver their estimated value.
- 10 per cent reduction in project cost overruns.
- Faster time to market by reducing project duration by 10 per cent.
- Fewer low-value and redundant projects by cancelling 10 to 20 per cent.
- 10 to 15 per cent decrease in the amount of resources dedicated to projects.

#3: The sponsor is both advocate and accountable

Top management's recognition of the need for change is not enough to successfully carry out the transformation. What is also necessary is top management's leadership of, and active involvement in, this initiative.

The sponsor of the project has to be either the company's CEO (preferably) or the equivalent, such as the COO or the CFO. First, they need to believe that projects and project management are a key competency for the organization's future. Second, the sponsor needs to dedicate time to steer and drive the transformation. By time I mean at least half a day per week, if not more. They need to actively participate in the key meetings, engage key stakeholders in supporting and resourcing the initiative.

Once you have established a sense of urgency and appointed the project sponsor, you need to move to selection of a project leader. They should be one of the best and most skilful members of the organization rather than someone who is simply readily available. If necessary, the project leader could be an external consultant, someone who has already successfully delivered such a transformation. Selecting someone from outside the organization often works better because they can directly confront the pockets of resistance without being biased or influenced by internal agendas. As resistance levels are sometimes high, you'll need to address critical issues as a matter of urgency, and it is important that the project leader be persuasive and unafraid of expressing views that differ from those of top management. Finally, it is imperative that the project leader be 120 per cent dedicated to the project.

#4: Customer needs drive the solution

There are many customers of the 10 Principles. Some are internal, such as the executive team (who are ultimately accountable that the project is implemented successfully) and the project manager (who will need to learn and be the first to apply the new ways of working). But also the businesses and functions that will benefit from better and faster projects. All these internal customers should be involved in sharing their needs and views on how the 10 Principles can be adapted and implemented. And don't forget the Board of Directors, they should also have a say in what they expect from the transformation project.

If your organization is providing services and executing projects for the government and other companies, consider involving some of them in the discussions and the identification of needs at the outset; at least take soundings from your key clients.

Remember that both internal and external client needs will evolve over time; include regular check points with them to ensure the outcome of the project is still in line with their new expectations.

#5: Realistic planning involves both ambition and pragmatism

Set an ambitious deadline. On average, the timescale for implementing the 10 Principles and becoming a project-driven organization can be two to three years. I recommend you go for a more challenging goal, make it happen in nine to twelve months. The longer the project, the harder it is to keep people motivated and the executive team supportive.

To kick off, the project leader and the sponsor will share the high-level project plan that identifies key milestones and primary workstreams. A significant part of the plan is dedicated to activities that support the change in the organization. Once the project nears completion, but before the changes are put into operation, a transitional plan should be set up.

The implementation will generate two different types of costs:

- transformation project costs (employees, consultants, training and eventually software purchase), and
- costs to run the new organization.

The benefits of implementing the new ways of working, as stated in Principle #2, will largely absorb the investment (transformation) cost.

#6: The perfect is the enemy of the good

One of the biggest challenges when implementing the new structure and capabilities to lead projects is to enforce use of the new methods and tools. Several project management-related processes, templates and tools will be deployed that will change the way people work. These new standards will temporarily increase the workload; and right from the start, employees will resist following them

The resistance to change leads to a suboptimal implementation of the principles and best practices, impacting the ultimate quality of the work done.

Successful organizations don't sacrifice on quality. On the contrary, they embrace excellence as one of their core values. Management must lead by example and be the first ones applying the new concepts and setting a high-level standard. The project team should also be disciplined and ensure the best quality is delivered in terms of support and communication to make the implementation of the 10 Principles a success.

#7: Well-managed uncertainty is a source of advantage

What are the major risks in the transformation journey? As with any large business transformation, it entails significant probable risks that the project team need to actively monitor and eventually mitigate. These are the most important of these risks.

- **Weakened top management support**
  Top management's attention and support are not unlimited. If the transformation encounters major resistance and the benefits take longer to be achieved, top management support will fade away.

- **Opposition to implementing the new organizational and governing structure**
  The organizational changes brought are brutal. Significant power, some resources and portions of the budget will shift from the run-the-business to the change-the-business dimension.

- **Resistance to increasing transparency and sharing information**

Transparency is very uncomfortable for some managers because it brings important information to the surface, such as the status of some projects or bad decision making, and allows top management to assess and compare individual managers' capabilities. This results in a huge 'invisible' resistance to becoming transparent, which top management needs to counter by being firm and advocating transparency's benefits.

#8: Stakeholder involvement is required and continual

To ensure that the 10 Principles are fully embraced by your organization, it is of the utmost importance that stakeholders are identified and fully engaged. To achieve that, perform a stakeholder analysis meeting with the project core team and the sponsor. Find those individuals that are keen to support the new ways of working (usually your project community will be very positive and supportive about this initiative). Identify also those individuals that might be resistant to change. Remember that resistance is often overcome by involvement and active listening. Lastly, seek out highly influential people (often senior leaders, but not always); by having them on board, your transformation project will benefit from quick decisions, enough resources and budget.

Once you have performed the stakeholder analysis, develop a communications and change management plan. Extensive training, and not only for the project teams, but also for the senior leaders, will be required too.

#9: A high-performing team and culture are indicators of the health and resilience of a project

As soon as the project leader has been appointed, the rest of the project team should be selected. The core team might include five to eight people who are also full time on the project, as well as functional and technical experts from each affected department who will:

- share best practices
- participate in defining methodologies
- validate the processes and the tools, and then
- lead the adoption of the new model in their business units.

These departmental representatives need to dedicate at least 50 per cent of their time to the project.

Remember that the most engaged members of a project are often those who voluntarily join the project; they have already connected with the purpose of the project, and believe they can contribute to making it a success.

Set time aside with the team to discuss the team's identity and ground rules. Use the checklist provided in Chapter 12 to ensure all the elements are taken into account. Creating a high-performing team can often be the reason for success, rather than failure.

#10: Project-driven organizations build capability to deliver change

The 10 Principles of Project Success transformation must be close to the top of the priority list of company endeavours. It should not be the first and most important, because that position should always be filled by a strategic project related directly to revenue growth or profitability.

If the business, as is likely, does not rank its projects formally, through a portfolio management process, a good indication of project importance is the amount of time that top management dedicates to the project and the level of the sponsor and the members of the steering committee within the organizational hierarchy.

Conclusion

Increasing your awareness of projects and understanding the 10 Principles is not an easy journey. It takes some time to reap the benefits, but it is definitely worth it. In fact, as we have seen, for many organizations having people who really understand projects is a matter of survival.

Once you have completed the transformation project, your organization is in a position to apply and exploit the 10 Principles at the heart of this book.

Your organization will have more clarity on strategic projects and how to implement them. Not only that, but applying the 10 Principles will bring the agility required to react faster to moves by the competition and to market opportunities.

Your employees will see more possibilities to grow and develop, increasing their engagement and contribution to the long-term success of your organization. You and your management team will become leaders in the new project economy.

As an individual, you now have the tools to turn your ideas into a reality. Make sure you incorporate them into your daily routines. If you do, you'll certainly be more successful with your projects, both professional and personal.

Good luck on your journey!

Endnotes

(All websites listed in the notes were accessed in March 2019.)

1. The emergence of projects

1   Josh Bersin, 'Catch the wave: The 21st-century career', *Deloitte Review*, issue 21, 31 July 2017.

2   Amy X. Wang, 'The number of Americans working for themselves could triple by 2020', *Quartz at Work*, 21 February 2018.

3   https://www.gpm-ipma.de/know_how/studienergebnisse/ makrooekonomische_vermessung_der_projekttaetigkeit_in_ deutschland.html.

2. What are projects?

1   See 'An iconic, world-first infrastructure project in South West Wales' at http://www.tidallagoonpower.com/projects/ swansea-bay/.

2   Frederick Winslow Taylor (1856–1915), see https://www.bl.uk/ people/frederick-winslow-taylor.

3   Henry Ford (1863–1947), see https://www.britannica.com/ biography/Henry-Ford.

4   Igor Ansoff (1918–2002), see https://www.business.com/articles/ management-theory-of-igor-ansoff/.

5   Peter Drucker (1909–2005), see https://www.business.com/articles/ management-theory-of-peter-drucker-key-terms/.

6   Michael Porter (1947–), see https://www.isc.hbs.edu/about-michael-porter/biography/Pages/default.aspx.

3. Reinventing project management

1   IBM Corporation, 'Making Change Work', 2008; for a full version of this paper visit ibm.com/gbs/makingchangework.

2   https://www.geneca.com/why-up-to-75-of-software-projects-will-fail/.

3   Nadim F. Matta and Ronald N. Ashkenas, 'Why Good Projects Fail Anyway', *Harvard Business Review*, September 2003.

4   Zoltán Kovács, 'The Budapest M4 metro: a study in inefficiency and waste', *Budapest Beacon*, 29 March 2014.

5   https://www.msn.com/en-in/money/photos/13-billion-dollar-projects-that-didnt-last-the-distance/ss-AAzsxlf#image=2.

6   Sean Martin, 'Is the $150bn International Space Station the most expensive scientific flop in history?', *Express*, 25 February 2016.

7   Nicole Gelinas, 'Lessons of Boston's Big Dig', *City Journal*, Autumn 2007.

8   Virginia Greiman, 'The Big Dig: Learning from a Mega Project', NASA *ASK Magazine*, 15 July 2010.

9   Pierre L. Gosselin, 'Wall Street Journal Calls Merkel's Energiewende "A Meltdown" Involving "Astronomical Costs"', NoTricksZone, 19 November 2017.

10 See https://www.kickstarter.com/help/stats: this page is automatically updated daily with the raw data behind Kickstarter.

11 Full research and more details can be found in my book *The Focused Organization: How Concentrating on a Few Key Initiatives Can Dramatically Improve Strategy Execution*, Gower, 2012.

12 See my books *The Focused Organization*, Gower, 2012; *The Project Revolution*, LID, 2019.

13 Bank of England figures for GDP evolution from 1900 to 2010.

14 Jethro Mullen and Charles Riley, 'End of the superjumbo: Airbus is giving up on the A380', CNN Business, 14 February 2019.

15 https://www.mckinsey.com/featured-insights/performance-transformation/five-fifty-ultralarge.

4. Principle #1: Everything starts with ideation

1   Visit http://theleanstartup.com/, the official website of entrepreneur Eric Ries.

2   https://www.ihs.com/products/telecommunication-market.html.

3   Brian Merchant, *The One Device: The Secret History of the iPhone*, Bantam Press, 2017.

4   https://www.phonearena.com/news/Did-you-know-that-the-first-iTunes-phone-presented-by-Steve-Jobs-was-not-an-iPhone_id56973.

5   http://www.investopedia.com/articles/investing/052115/how-why-google-glass-failed.asp.

6   https://exponents.co/product-marketing-google-glass/.

7   http://bgr.com/2015/06/27/google-glass-epic-fail-what-happened/.

8   http://monetizinginnovation.com/2016/04/the-reason-google-glass-failed/.

5. Principle #2: A clear purpose informs and inspires

1   Rupa Haria, 'Concorde Prototypes In Production (1967)', *Aviation Week & Space Technology*, 7 May 2015.

2   Ken Niles, 'The Hanford cleanup: What's taking so long?', *Bulletin of the Atomic Scientists*, 1 July 2014.

3   NAO, 'The Channel Tunnel Rail Link', report by the Comptroller and Auditor General, HC302 Session 2000–2001, 28 March 2001.

4   http://theconversation.com/explainer-how-panama-canal-expansion-will-transform-shipping-once-again-61490.

5   Jim Collins and Jerry I. Porras, *Built to Last: Successful Habits of Visionary Companies*, Harper Business, 1997.

6   Rob Jones and Richard Davies, 'Vision, Mission and Values', micro-report on Crossrail's learning legacy, 27 September 2016, see https://www.majorprojectsknowledgehub.net/resources/vision-mission-values/.

7   Author of *Start with Why: How Great Leaders Inspire Everyone to Take Action* (Penguin Books, 2011) and *The Infinite Game: How Great Businesses Achieve Long-Lasting Success* (Penguin Books, 2019); YouTube interview, 'Simon Sinek Explains What Almost Every Leader Gets Wrong'.

8   Personal communication with the author. Visit Jeroen De Flander's website at https://jeroen-de-flander.com/.

9   Personal communication with the author. Visit Anders Indset's website at https://www.businessphilosopher.com/.

10 George T. Doran, 'There's a S.M.A.R.T. way to write management's goals and objectives', *Management Review* (70), November 1981.

6. Principle #3: The sponsor is both advocate and accountable

1   See Ron Ashkenas, 'How to Be an Effective Executive Sponsor', *Harvard Business Review*, 18 May 2015, for some good insights into the expectations for the role.

2   NAO, 'The failure of the FiReControl project', report by the Comptroller and Auditor General, HC 1272 Session 2010–2012, 1 July 2011.

3   Jose Maria Delos Santos, 'Understanding Responsibility Assignment Matrix (RACI Matrix)', project-management. com, 20 November 2018, at https://project-management.com/understanding-responsibility-assignment-matrix-raci-matrix/.

7. Principle #4: Customer needs drive the solution

1   Phil Driver, *Validating Strategies: Linking Projects and Results to Uses and Benefits*, Routledge, 2016.

2   NAO, 'The cost-effective delivery of an armoured vehicle capability', report by the Comptroller and Auditor General, HC1029 Session 2010–2012, 20 May 2011.

3   https://www.news24.com/Archives/City-Press/Nelson-Mandela-Bay-buses-worth-R100m-gather-dust-in-failed-project-20150429.

4   https://www.designbuild-network.com/projects/bbc-redevelopment/.

5   NAO, 'The BBC's management of three major estate projects', report by the Comptroller and Auditor General presented to the BBC Trust's Finance and Compliance Committee, 13 January 2010.

6   You can follow the progress of Star Citizen online at: https://robertsspaceindustries.com/funding-goals.

7   https://www.uxdesignagency.com/blog/UI_UX_concept_of_mobile_only_challenger_bank_from_UX_Design_Agency.

8. Principle #5: Realistic planning involves both ambition and pragmatism

1 https://exploredia.com/top-10-most-expensive-projects-in-history-of-mankind.

2 David Gritten, 'Boyhood: Richard Linklater interview', *Daily Telegraph*, 9 February 2015.

9. Principle #6: The perfect is the enemy of the good

1 Calleam Consulting Ltd, 'Denver International Airport Baggage Handling System – An illustration of ineffectual decision making', report published in 2008.

2 https://www.royalhaskoningdhv.com/en-gb/united-kingdom/projects/offering-integrated-project-management-for-heathrow-terminal-3/5263.

3 https://www.designingbuildings.co.uk/wiki/Building_Services_Validation.

4 Brian Merchant, *The One Device: The Secret History of the iPhone*, Bantam Press, 2017.

5 https://www.pmi.org/pmbok-guide-standards.

6 ISO 9000, clause 3.2.10.

7 ISO 9000, clause 3.2.11.

10. Principle #7: Well-managed uncertainty is a source of advantage

1 https://assets.publishing.service.gov.uk/media/54c1704ce5274a15b6000025/FormalInvestigation_HeraldofFreeEnterprise-MSA1894.pdf.

2 Kim Willsher, 'French railway operator SNCF orders hundreds of new trains that are too big', *Guardian*, 21 May 2014.

11. Principle #8: Stakeholder involvement is required and continual

1 https://www.computerweekly.com/news/252457423/IR35-reforms-Contractors-lack-confidence-in-private-sector-to-manage-April-2020-rule-change.

2 https://www.majorprojectsknowledgehub.net/resources/tunnelling-barbican-engaging-stakeholders/.

3   Highways England, 'A303 Stonehenge: Amesbury to Berwick Down', preliminary environmental information report, February 2018.

4   Alan Hope, 'Uplace shopping and leisure centre loses its building permit – is this the end?', *Brussels Times*, 10 October 2018.

5   https://www.pmi.org/pmbok-guide-standards/foundational/pmbok.

6   https://www.pmi.org/learning/thought-leadership/pulse/ pulse-of-the-profession-2016.

7   https://ec.europa.eu/easme/en/communication-toolkit.

12. Principle #9: A high-performing team and culture are indicators of the health and resilience of a project

1   Personal communication with the author. Visit Marshall Goldsmith's website at https://www.marshallgoldsmith.com/.

2   https://coaa.org/Documents/Owner-Resources/Industry-Resources/IPD-for-Public-and-Private-Owners.aspx.

3   https://www.meetingquality.com/about-us.html.

4   https://www.theverge.com/2017/6/13/15782200/one-device-secret-history-iphone-brian-merchant-book-excerpt.

5   Brian Merchant, *The One Device: The Secret History of the iPhone*, Bantam Press, 2017.

13. Principle #10: Project-driven organizations build capability to deliver change

1   https://www.businessinsider.com/. how-lego-made-a-huge-turnaround-2014-2?r=US&IR=T.

2   https://ec.europa.eu/info/law/law-topic/data-protection_en.

3   Antonio Nieto-Rodriguez, 'How to Prioritize Your Company's Projects', *Harvard Business Review*, 13 December 2016.

4   www.ipma.world/chief-project-officer-cpo-new-role-project-oriented-organisations/.

14. From project manager to project leader

1   Lao-Tzu, *Tao Te Ching*, Hackett Publishers, 1712.

2   See, for example: 'Behavioral Theories of Leadership' at https://www.leadership-central.com/behavioral-theories.html; 'The

Fundamentals of Level 5 Leadership' at https://lesley.edu/article/the-fundamentals-of-level-5-leadership.

3 www.praxisframework.org/en/ima/four-colours-general.

4 https://www.ipma.world/assets/IPMA-Code-of-Ethics-and-Professional-Conduct.pdf.

15. Start thriving with your projects

1 Most of these figures are based on the Forrester Research 2009 Annual Report.

Acknowledgements

I dedicate this book to my family. My wonderful wife and partner, Clarisse, with her unconditional support; my superb children – Laura, Alexander, Selma and Lucas; my caring parents – Maria Jose and Juan Antonio; and my cool brothers – Javi, Iñaki y Jose Miguel.

I would like to especially thank Jonathan Norman, who believed in my first book in 2012 and has been instrumental throughout the entire editorial process. Also, grateful to Stuart Crainer, from Thinkers50, for his ever-inspirational advice; and Martina O'Sullivan, and her team from Penguin, for her trust in asking me to author for their new business series.

Lastly, I want to dedicate this book to the millions of project managers with their hard work – often unrecognized – that contributes every day to make a better world.

Index